PRAISE FOR *AND STILL SHE LAUGHS*

"Kate's book is as comfortable as a coffee date with your best friend but as spiritually insightful as getting a masters in theology. She weaves together the stories of unsung women in the Bible with her own hard-won lessons of grace in the midst of suffering. These pages are a reminder that the story of God's love in the world has been, and continues to be, written through the stories of our lives, especially the ones we would never have written for ourselves."

—Katherine Wolf, coauthor of *Hope Heals*

"Christians tend to be known for their answers. I'm so proud of my friend Kate, for being honest about the questions that come with grief. She invites us to join her as she wrestles with God and goes looking for hope. And it needs to be said: Kate Merrick can straight-up write."

—Jamie Tworkowski, founder of To Write Love on
Her Arms and author of *If You Feel Too Much*

"Kate Merrick is one of those women that I always wish I had more time with—her honesty, sincerity, and messy straightforwardness are different, in the very best way. Her book, *And Still She Laughs*, is the same way. It's one of those books I will keep coming back to for truth and inspiration."

—Lindsey Nobles, COO of the IF:Gathering

"Where do you turn when your worst nightmare comes true? How do you hold onto faith? With spunk and vibrant honesty, Kate shares her story of suffering and loss—and her incredible journey to a great joy restored. Whatever pain life has brought you, inside these pages waits your holy invitation to laugh loud once more."

—Allison Trowbridge, author of *Twenty-Two*

"*And Still She Laughs* is the terrifying, tearful, heartbreaking, heart-healing, humorous, and definitive true story of survival and triumph. Amid an unimaginable journey of love and loss, Kate Merrick shares the beautiful and brief life of her beloved daughter, Daisy, and her victory over the cancer that claimed the mortality of her precious eight year old."

—Kathy Ireland, chair of Kathy Ireland Worldwide

"*And Still She Laughs* moves the reader beyond surface talk and plumbs to the depths of Kate's heart and God's word to present the reality of how God works in the dark edges and billowing sorrows of life to bring healing, wholeness, and yes—joy! With rank honesty, touches of humor, and deep insights, Kate shares the gemstones mined from the dark caverns of her life. No Bible passage is merely skimmed or receives an honorable mention. It is obvious that each story has been hashed out, thought out, and lived out in Kate's life. Personally, I plan on keeping my office stacked with this book to share with the women who visit me to 'talk.' It is a compelling, insightful, and, at times, engagingly raw account of how true spirituality is lived out in a fallen world. I loved every word on every page!"

> —Cheryl Brodersen, author of *When a Woman Chooses to Forgive*

"Kate Merrick not only has the extraordinary ability to share about suffering in a way that gives a voice to our own, but also to point us toward the one hope for it. With wisdom, wit, and refreshing honesty, Kate invites us to a faith without illusions, displayed in the stories of scripture and rooted in a crucified yet risen savior."

> —Tim Chaddick, founding pastor of RealityLA, lead pastor for Reality Church London, and author of *Better* and *The Truth about Lies*

"Kate Merrick is a living, breathing example of how we can all go from lamenting to laughing again."

> —Esther Fleece, author of *No More Faking Fine*

"If you've endured pain and trauma, you will know how lonely loss can make you feel. Where do we go? What do we do? I love how Kate boldly and honestly dares us to laugh in moments when we feel unable to. As her story unfolds, she reveals the hope that is found behind pain, beauty in the midst of ashes, and laughter that is heard in the wake of sadness. She, like Paul the Apostle, teaches us to scream in the midst of loss, 'O death where is your victory?'"

> —Bianca Juarez Olthoff, chief storyteller for A21 and bestselling author of *Play with Fire*

"If there was ever a title that captured the life and witness of the author, it's my dear friend's book: *And Still She Laughs*. This book ministered to me so deeply. Guys, I recommend you buy this for a woman you love and then ask to borrow it!"

> —Dave Lomas, author of *The Truest Thing About You*

and
Still
She
Laughs

and Still She Laughs

DEFIANT JOY IN THE DEPTHS OF SUFFERING

kate merrick

NELSON
BOOKS

An Imprint of Thomas Nelson

Published in Nashville, Tennessee, by Nelson Books, an imprint of Thomas Nelson. Nelson Books and Thomas Nelson are registered trademarks of HarperCollins Christian Publishing, Inc.

Published in association with the literary agency of D. C. Jacobson & Associates, LLC, an Author Management Company, www.dcjacobson.com.

Thomas Nelson titles may be purchased in bulk for educational, business, fundraising, or sales promotional use. For information, please e-mail SpecialMarkets@ ThomasNelson.com.

ISBN 978-0-7180-9309-9 (eBook)

Library of Congress Cataloging-in-Publication Data

ISBN 978-0-7180-9281-8
Names: Merrick, Kate, 1974- author.
Title: And still she laughs : defiant joy in the depths of suffering / Kate Merrick.
Description: Nashville : Thomas Nelson, 2017.
Identifiers: LCCN 2016036961 | ISBN 9780718092818
Subjects: LCSH: Children--Death--Religious aspects--Christianity. |
 Consolation. | Mothers--Religious life. | Merrick, Kate, 1974-
Classification: LCC BV4907 .M47 2017 | DDC 248.8/66092--dc23 LC record available at https://lccn.loc.gov/2016036961

Printed in the United States of America

17 18 19 20 21 LSC 10 9 8 7 6 5 4 3 2

For Britt: We did it. You and me.
We survived, and I love you more than ever.

CONTENTS

"She is clothed with strength and dignity,
and she laughs without fear of the future."
—Proverbs 31:25

INTRODUCTION

There's a bird's nest just outside my house filled with a family of chicks. I love to watch what's going on in the life of my bird family. Little bald babies make little *peep peep* noises. The mama bird works tirelessly, flitting back and forth, always taking care of her puny chicks who are smashed together in their gross nest caked with droppings. She's amazing. As she's giving her little ones what they need, day by day the chicks grow less helpless, less scrawny, less ugly. They are slowly becoming strong and beautiful.

As I was watching this real-life nature program the other day and musing on the stillness of a California evening in the country, I realized that often I feel like one of those baby birds. All scrawny and weak and featherless and pathetic, unable to get my own nourishment, mouth open wide, crying for something, anything. There I am, sitting in shambles, poop everywhere, unable to fly, crying out for something to get me through—to move me beyond this state of helplessness. Jesus has been to me like that mama bird: taking care of me, feeding me tirelessly while I'm sitting scared and stuck. Day by day he helps me to grow shiny feathers until I become nourished by truth and ready to fly.

Real life has proven strange. There has been tragedy and comedy, defeat and victory. I'm pretty sure it's not what I signed up for, pretty sure I got someone else's lot. But after pinching myself nice and hard, I am assured that this is indeed my life. No, my soul is not trapped in the body of another. This is my actual body. This is my actual life. So what shall I do? I shall look up, open my mouth, and allow my All Sufficient One to feed my soul. Looking to the Source, I shall rejoice with laughing and mourn with weeping. I shall give from my emptiness; I shall receive the offer of abundance. And I shall keep right on going, moving ahead in life, taking steps of faith, and keeping my eyes on the One who is invisible—who has, in his generosity and continuous provision like that mama bird, taught me to laugh without fear of the future.

One

AND SUCH IS LIFE

The days and weeks following Daisy's earthly departure were of a strange sort. Hovering in our home was an empty feeling, much like when a door slams shut in your face. You feel the rush of air forcing your hair back for a brief moment, then a wall directly in front of you, so close up that everything else is out of focus. We sat around that first day, drinking coffee and looking about the room, blinking for lack of recognition of our surroundings. We said good-bye to her in the night, and sat in the darkness together as the remnants of the gloomy wee hours surrendered to the gradual appearing of the winter sun.

I found myself staring into nothing, moving sloth-like, actions and words suspended in midair—both requiring more effort than I could afford. All drive had been released from me, like a burst tire. I was flat, slow, nearly useless.

Death had come for my daughter. The words made no sense. To me they sounded like a different language. One I didn't know. *Death. Dead. Deceased.* I couldn't compute. I couldn't understand it. I couldn't grasp how she was here chattering in her sleep just hours ago, and so I stared.

Hours passed in our living room, where family joined us in the sorrow. It's too strenuous to look someone in the eye during times like this, so I fixated on a stray fiber in the rug, refilled my mug, found reasons to close my eyes for extended periods. Maybe it would all disappear.

After the initial blow settled in, there crept up in me an amplified hatred of all things that reminded me of Daisy's cancer treatment and subsequent suffering. In a frenzied, brief burst I rid my home of all medical paraphernalia. I hastily threw away all bandages, needles, sharps containers, medications, tubes, pumps, and alcohol wipes, shoving them deep into the trash can, slamming down the lid. What I couldn't throw away, I stashed out of sight while we waited for the medical supply truck to pick it up: various machines for pumping drugs into Daisy's veins, a commode, a tiny wheelchair. The very sight of these accoutrements of torture turned my stomach, and they couldn't be gotten rid of quickly enough.

Toward the afternoon, I spent some time in her tiny bed that had been at the foot of our large one: the one she died in, the one we crowded together on as a family while we cuddled her empty body in the night, while we said our last good-byes as a family of four. It was an old pine bed my dad had built for me when I was a toddler. Daisy had still been so small she fit perfectly in it, like a little mouse in a pocket. The bedsheets smelled of her, and I wanted to breathe as deeply as possible, as if the act would magically bring her back.

The following day, though, Britt and I dismantled the

bed. We knew that if we didn't, we would both continue to lie there individually, folding our bodies into the last place she had breathed, unwilling to accept the truth. It would become an idol to us, an altar of suffering, a pitiful attempt to keep things the way they were and not let them out of our desperate grip.

After the house was rid of physical reminders of the toll cancer takes, I was left fumbling with my hands— empty arms that for twelve years straight had been busy holding babies, making messes with preschoolers, or caring for my cancer-riddled daughter. I felt naked, exposed, and strangely self-conscious. The fight had ended, and I was the loser.

Days went by, all melded together. How does one go through the motions of life when death has swept through your world? It was like trying to speak, but emitting barely a squeak; trying to walk, but wading through quicksand; trying to breathe, but choking on life.

C. S. Lewis says in *A Grief Observed*,

Grief still feels like fear. Perhaps, more strictly, like suspense. Or like waiting; just hanging about waiting for something to happen. It gives life a permanently provisional feeling. It doesn't seem worth starting anything. I can't settle down. I yawn, I fidget, I smoke too much. Up till this I always had too little time. Now there is nothing but time. Almost pure time, empty successiveness.

I felt suspended, waiting, helpless, incredibly self-conscious in those early days. The awkwardness has taken a few years to subside.

Like a pair of old jeans with a memory of its own, that once fit every curve, I had to relinquish life as I knew it before Daisy left for heaven. I had to get used to a new pair, a new life. A new pair with different faded spots, different belt loops, different worn parts. No longer a family of four, we had become a family of three. No longer a balanced bunch, I had become the only girl in the house. No longer a crusader for healing, I had become a bereaved mom. No longer Daisy's best friend and fiercest defender, I had been stripped of my immediate mission. Instead I became bored and lonely. They fit now, this new pair of jeans, this new life without her. They fit. Though I want my old jeans back.

And yet, though hollow in the missing of one of its crucial members, my house is filled with gifts. Gifts that speak to me when I'm uncomfortable in my own skin, when I'd rather leave and never come back. The toy mouse she hid by the stairs to frighten unsuspecting passersby, complete with a mouse hole made from construction paper. A grocery list in the drawer—all her favorites written in her quirky spelling style—*keewee, rut beer, q-cumbers*. Her tiny leopard-print leggings folded on the dryer, each glance I give them flooding me with memories of the way she looked in them—a tiny booty and bird legs, sticking out from underneath tie-dye. And the graffiti. My darling angel would draw a pile of poop surrounded with buzzing flies or an anchor-tattooed, hairy-chested princess on her grammar worksheets, sufficiently raising the bar on inappropriate artwork. Once in a while I run across a tragically moving journal entry she wrote, hopeful and optimistic for the future. But really, anything she wrote is my favorite, because not only did she touch the paper, but what was tucked in her heart came out onto the page. Though Daisy is gone, she left love notes at every turn. It has taken two years to go through the things in her room, two searing years of a little here, a bit there.

I look for these little treasures every day. From time to time I run into something new and enjoy the memory flood, no matter what type of tears it brings. It's a weightless feeling, walking through grief. The body still needs food and sleep, the house still needs to be cleaned, the family still needs attention. It's almost like there is such a deluge of emotion all the time, it's easier to shut it out and become a zombie of sorts just to get on with the necessaries of life. I may be robotically going through the motions, yet when I happen upon a treasure, I experience a brief spark of life.

Even so, God has provided. He didn't leave me to grieve alone—I have a family who suffered the same loss. And in his kindness and generosity, he gave me the gift of another daughter to wrap my arms around. The gift of someone new to love, a diversion for the family, a little someone to care for in her sister's glaring absence. A generous gift.

I don't journal much, but I found this entry I wrote while I was pregnant and still reeling from loss:

There is a stretching pain both in my heart and in my body. The kind that pulls the fibers so thin that some of them snap, finding refuge in the curling, hiding where they came from. Most waking moments, sometimes hours, are spent wondering at the audacity that life goes on, remembering what has happened to my Daisy, feeling simultaneous pain and hope, depth of belief. Yet the breaking and retreating of various fibers of my soul are not quite ready to be grown to this point, not ready to carry the weight of the life gone from this world into the next. The life of my girl, whom I love so much, whom I can't see anymore, touch anymore, who is not dependent on me anymore.

Yet I believe God gives me glimpses into her existence, an existence I won't understand until our flesh embraces once again. One of possible time and space, of flesh as we know it, and of what is visible to the eyes God has given us. Strange, that the fibers of my soul should mirror the fibers of my body, growing, stretching, painfully preparing to carry the weight of new life. A life that is dependent upon me for oxygen, food, even elimination.

There is new life inside me, already mixed with aching and joy and wonder. A life that will give us new reason to love, to sacrifice, to share. A girl to bring joy and brightness, to give us opportunities to laugh, pray, cry. As certain as we are that we will hold the little one making her home in my womb, we will hold the little one who has made her home in heaven.

As my heart and body go through conflicting changes—heavier, lighter, made stronger, weak fibers tearing, making room for love, pouring out and being poured into, wondering, praying, moving in the realm of God's provision—one thing is certain. In the midst of darkness, in the still gray of dreariness, in the depths of sorrow, God has given us sunshine.

And such is life. A mixture of sunshine and rain, mountains and valleys, births and deaths. When Job's wife suggested he curse God and die, he responded with something simple but so profound: "Should we accept only good things from the hand of God and never anything bad?" (Job 2:10). It was time to walk in everything God had destined for us, and to do it with guts.

You know how sometimes we convince ourselves we are the only souls to walk the earth who have ever _____? You fill in the blank. Been cheated on?

Been stolen from? Been abused? Lost a child? Personally, I know the drama can escalate when I'm self-focused to the point of believing no one else has ever even had a pimple, much less a bad day. We too often make ourselves the center of the universe. That's exhausting.

Being around someone like that is incredibly annoying, and slowly but surely, I have come to realize I am that annoying person. God is dealing with me and giving me a restored perspective. He has informed me that, no, I'm not the only woman on the planet to experience such heartache. There are plenty more, an entire community of women who have suffered, perhaps even more so than I. News flash to me.

He is kindly leading me into a community of the suffering, and it's surprisingly comforting. Mortifying, but comforting, because in order to work through stuff we have to be aware of it first. I have been known to point out the speck in another's eye while there was a giant sequoia in my own. Oops.

The community of suffering is a heroic bunch. A strong, effective, hilarious, rock-solid bunch I would be honored to be lumped in with when I grow up, although on the surface it doesn't seem like the best of company. After all, the community I'm talking about consists of a woman who was used for sex, and whose infant son died. There's a woman with a reputation as an adulterer and deluded liar, who witnessed her son's brutal murder.

There's a woman who slept with her boss's husband and got pregnant, and there is a rich old lady known for laughing at inappropriate times, as well as getting busted for lying.

I'm talking about Bathsheba; Mary, the mother of Jesus; Hagar; and Sarah, the wife of Abraham. Women who suffered. Women who made a difference. Women like me and you. God surprised me with these lives of faith and, using them as guides, gently walked me through the years following Daisy's departure. These women's stories are filled with pain, yes, but thankfully also with honesty. Honesty that is crucial to healing, crucial to repentance, crucial to walking tall and strong.

Remarkably, I have gained an appreciation for suffering. Not in a sick, masochistic way, or even as a desperate undertaking for attention, but in a clearer understanding of the deeper things. Things like love, faith, eternity. I have learned not to fear suffering, because it's not my enemy but my teacher. I've encountered a deeper love of God than I thought possible, like a marriage that weathers the storm—both souls grateful to have held each other tight while the ship heaved unsteadily. Beauty is seen more crisply than ever before through the eye of the sufferer; gifts are heartily received and rejoiced over by the one who is able to take what is given. I never thought I'd say it, but suffering has been life-giving for me. I just never recognized it before.

God has taken me from that inability to move, that zombielike existence, to one of fullness of joy, one of dancing feet and swinging arms. Come with me while we uproot the plank from my eye—while I display the cards I've been holding too closely to my chest. I pray you find some comfort in my community, that you can let down your guard.

It's time.

Two

TINY PINE BOX

You know, it's funny. No, not ha-ha funny, but "I just came out of the church bathroom with the back of my skirt tucked into my undies and now the entire congregation has seen my unfortunate nethers on the way back to my seat" funny. A euphemism for something rotten. Rotten occurrences that come frequently—like a pattern that seems sickeningly typical of my life.

Remember the birds I told you about? Well, what I didn't tell you was that just as those darling birds were almost grown, almost ready to leave their smelly but precious nest, I went out to check on them. I was feeling lighthearted that morning, glad to be alive, grateful to be free and, well, feeling like things were going my way for once in a really long time. It was one of those days when you begin to forget the past heartaches and some of the present troubles, a day when you see fit to be brave and take a chance on life. Sun shining, deep breath of ranch air in my lungs, I was feeling perky in my pretty jammies and a messy bun.

So, chai tea in an Anthropologie *K* mug in hand, I checked on my feathered friends. I couldn't see them over the edge of the nest, so I kept moving closer to get a better look. Just a little closer . . . One more foot . . . So excited to get a glimpse of these delicate creatures God had kindly placed in my life. I inched up on my tiptoes, enjoying the warmth of the mug and of a pretty morning, of life. Convinced my birds knew and loved me and desired me to come hear them sing a personal concert, I was shocked when they popped their itty-bitty fuzzy heads up and looked at me in panic.

All three freaked out and jumped out of the nest, frantically flapping their adolescent, partially grown wings. Unable to fly. They landed in the nearby lime tree, and that's where they stayed, eyes wild, huffing and puffing their tiny bird chests. There was nothing I could do. Their mother would reject them if they had my scent on them, and they couldn't make it back to their nest on their own. I had killed God's nature gift to me; theirs would be a drawn-out death of starvation and helplessness.

I felt so lame, so defeated. I had only been enjoying the little shred of beauty found in such a simple thing, innocently wanting to delight in the gifts God had placed about me. Then, just like that, I knocked them to their doom.

Too often the joys we experience are so fleeting, so small, so easily spent. Relationships end, homes burn, bills pile up. Seems like summer always comes to an abrupt halt, plopping us into the stark and hungry landscape of winter, when all we were expecting was endless warmth, endless green, endless fun. Life, real life, with all its complicated and unsavory problems, with all its precariously balanced departments, never fails to surprise.

And then we find ourselves questioning God when things go awry. We shout beneath the stars and in the darkness of our cars as we drive. Questions run down our cheeks, onto our bodies in the shower, and slip down the drain. But then more well up and hover just beneath the surface of our skin, looking for a way of escape, a satisfactory answer.

Why suffering, God? Why sin? Why are you letting them get away with this? Why such darkness? Why the crushing of dreams on a regular basis? And why me?

Silence.

I have yet to hear the reason why. Oh, I've heard "answers" from the well-meaning. Answers that leave me thirsty and malnourished, sickened, or downright angry. I've heard every cliché, every Bible verse taken out of context, every flimsy offering of comfort said hurriedly with hopes of plugging up neatly what is spilling out of every crack of my being; sloppy, messy, dangerous. Things carelessly thrown about, hoping to gloss over the whole soiled lot.

"The Lord gives and takes away!"

"So many will be saved from your testimony!"

"Isn't it great her suffering is over?"

"God is good all the time!"

"He has plans to prosper you!"

Piles and piles of answers.

But I haven't gotten an answer from God. In fact, at this point I'm pretty sure I won't get one until I see him face-to-face. I have searched Scripture, screamed until my throat was raw, turned the questions into a dirge, a lament, an empty wailing that evaporates into thin air. There is a reason why my God has not seen fit to reply to my very human questions. My best guess is that I am not ready for the answers.

My story is the kind of sad story we have all read on a random blog that a friend has told us about, eyes wide, voice subdued. It seems like we all know someone in crisis, a person we're rooting for. We secretly love the drama, feel invested in the outcome. We cheer and say how good God is when things go their way, and we pray on knees when they don't. It's Stuff That Happens to Other People; it's horrible, put-your-hand-on-your-chest-and-gasp stories we "could never handle." It's repelling and addicting, and close enough to feel the secondhand pain but far enough away to thank God it's not happening to us.

But, alas, it seems that this time around it was me. It was my family. I was the one with the cancer kid, the one whose blog you followed, the one who received your teddy bears and cards and prayers. I was the one who learned what an oncologist was and how to give an injection, who held handfuls of my daughter's silky blond hair as it fell out in clumps. I was the one who spent countless days and nights in a hospital room, cursing the incessantly beeping IV pole. I was the one who had to wake her twelve-year-old son in the middle of the night to tell him that his sister had gone to heaven.

Now I'm the bereaved mother you avoid in the aisles of Trader Joe's. I'm the one who has received puppy-dog-sad-face looks from countless well-meaning people, making me want to hide my head in the sand or pretend I don't notice. I'm the "unfortunate" who has weathered the kind of storm normal people do all they can to avoid. I'm the woman who handed her daughter's body over to men in suits in the predawn hours, who spoke at her daughter's funeral—the woman who, with every heartbeat, feels cruelly marauded by our enemy Death. The very thing Jesus wept over, roared at, and even experienced himself.

Grief is like a bathing suit. It fits every person differently. Some hang out a bit here, some a bit there. Some shouldn't leave the house with it showing, and others make it look fabulous. Some grieve privately, never inviting another soul in. You might never know how they really feel; you might start to think they have checked out or are callous and coldhearted. Others do it openly, blogging as therapy, sharing their tears because it feels cathartic, because they need to grieve in community.

How is anyone to know what to do, how to help, how

to survive? Some of the brokenhearted feel hurt if you don't ask after them, if you don't acknowledge their loss or their crisis. Others never want you to mention it, as if speaking of the lost loved one acknowledges the fact that he or she won't come back. What do you do? Do you "go there" with a hurting person? Do you risk the discomfort of snot and tears and a breakdown at the farmer's market or the coffee shop?

And then there's me.

In all honesty, I'm still not really ready to be open with grief. It feels like a water balloon, and if I spring a leak and let a little bit out, I might explode all over the place. I carefully keep these surges of sadness to myself, occasionally sharing them only with my husband, because they're private and sacred to me. But I'm trusting you with these things that I'm writing. I'm trusting God to do a good work in the sharing of human feelings, the acknowledgment that we are emotional, created for love. That being said, this book, fortunately, is not about me. It's about Jesus, the Most Beautiful. But I share my life because we learn from each other, we are relational beings, and, well, it's what I've got.

If at any time you feel like throwing this book across the room, then go for it. I have thrown many books across the room at different points in the last several years. It's actually quite satisfying to bark "Grow up!" at the author while the cover yawns open with pages ruffling willy-nilly until coming to a punctuated halt on the wall across from you. Harsh? Not really. Your story could be worse than mine. I mean, if you're reading this book and you have lost more than one child, do it now. Then go pick it back up. If you are still sitting in the ashes scratching your skin like Job, and if your grief is new and you aren't ready emotionally to look up, chuck it now. Then go pick it back up. If you have ongoing misery, if you have a painful disease, if you have any reason to grit your teeth because you don't feel happy or clappy, pitch it. Then go pick it back up. Not because I want you to listen to me blather on, but because Jesus is worth it. He's worth signing up for, worth staying married to. He's worth the effort, the tears, the doubt, the confusion of life.

This book is not intended to take the place of grieving; rather, it speaks to what to do when the tidal wave washes past, when the sizzle from the burn settles, when we finally look around and wonder what's next. When we wonder if it is actually possible to come out of the paralysis of darkness and find laughter again. Really find it—the deep sense of peace and joy that leans into faith and away from the fear your experiences tempt you to live in. I want you to know—whether you have weathered a tempest, whether you are currently wading knee-deep in sin, whether you are disappointed, disillusioned, or disgusted—laughter is for you. Whether you're nursing relational wounds, fastidiously covering up your self-inflicted scars, or if you're alive and have walked this earth long enough to stumble, crash, or burn, this is for you.

This book is not saying your life on earth doesn't matter. This book is not saying that you can never be sad. This book is not a manual on how to come through tragedy stronger than ever. This is not about how to be happy in ten easy steps. This is not a theological case for laughter, or why there is evil in the world, but rather how God has worked in my life and can work in yours too. I may not be a scholar, but I do know what I've experienced. I've read the testimonies of biblical women and gleaned truth from their very real and imperfect lives. And because Satan the accuser is defeated by the blood of the Lamb and the word of our testimonies (Rev. 12:11), I will offer mine.

I'll start at the beginning of the end. In September 2009, Daisy Love, my darling girl of five years old, was diagnosed with kidney cancer. It was a Monday, the third week of school. I was so excited that fall because for the first time in nine years I would have a bit of freedom. Both kids would be in school full-time and I had a fall bucket list all lined up. By far the best way I could think of spending that freedom, and what's always at the top of my list, was going surfing with my husband. He was a pastor and happened to have Mondays off, so we packed the car accordingly before we loaded up the kids for school.

It's mystifying to see the little ways God works in our lives. Sometimes it's a monumental, cosmically cool event, and other times it's as simple as the order of how things go in a day. On this Monday, we dropped off the kids and headed south on the freeway in Carpinteria, California, to Channel Islands, my husband's family's surfboard business. We headed into the factory to pick up a new board for Britt and a demo of a new model for me to try. My newfound liberation from mom duties that Monday made it fun to do even mundane-ish things, like hanging out in a dusty surfboard factory talking to old friends. Our loitering took longer than standard loitering usually does, and by the time we were back in the car and heading to the beach, we got a phone call—the call we would have missed if we had left sooner and headed straight for the water.

"Daisy has fallen down and is not feeling well. She is vomiting and in pain," our dear friend at the school said on the other end of the line. Daisy, our sunshine. Daisy, our creative and hilarious girl. Daisy, our freckled and funny and cool and kind and loving and full-of-life daughter. Hurt.

After many hours in the ER and myriad tests, the pediatric doctor in charge of her case called for an oncologist.

A nurse came in with a peculiar look on her face, setting down a box of tissues. I didn't know what an oncologist was, but I knew what the box of tissues was for. And so began the years of sickness, of physical and emotional agony, of soul-searching, of gut-wrenching real life. The kind I was convinced we were immune to.

While my son learned multiplication tables, my daughter had a massive tumor removed from her abdomen. While her friends went to birthday parties, Christmas cookie parties, and ski trips, Daisy went to the clinic for chemotherapy and home to vomit. While my friends decided which extracurricular activities would most benefit their little ones, I decided which beanie would most gently cover my little one's tender, naked scalp. While the rest of the world went to school and work—while life went on and plans were made—our family hunkered down. Our family washed our hands until they cracked, afraid of every germ. Our family was trapped in our home without visitors for fear of any virus that could kill my kindergartner, whose immune system had been obliterated by treatment. Our family counted on nothing further than today, when often the today was sketchy.

We spent three and a half years in treatment, three and a half years searching for a cure for the monster that kept coming back to take over Daisy's spare body. She had multiple invasive and dangerous surgeries, count-less sickening chemo treatments, and we fried her guts with daily radiation for weeks on end. We fed her sprouts and we juiced kale. We put her on a mostly low-sugar, organic, anti-cancer, grow-out-your-armpit-hair diet. We prayed and fasted and cried out desperately for healing, and when all else failed we traveled to Israel for three months seeking advanced experimental treatments. All to no avail. Her body was ravaged, ragged, full of tubes and patched together. It finally gave out altogether in February 2013, and she took her last breath in our arms. Her daddy and I overlapped with arms and legs and faces covered with tears and murmurs of loving words too holy to repeat.

In our bedroom in the deep of the night we held her reed-thin body, never wanting to let go. We pulled out all the horrid tubes and wrapped her in her favorite soft blanket. We covered her little bald head and wept and kissed her face over and over. Then, as we fell to our knees and worshipped God—who had given her to us and to whom she had gone—we felt the presence of angels and knew we were not alone.

I never want to do that again.

My life is forever changed, and I am forever changed. I have aged in this deep grief, this unknowable experience. I have grown tougher. I have become different. One of the differences in me has been hiding silently for a while. I don't know when this thing crept in, when I gave it a space to live, when I told it to pull up a chair and get comfy. This deceptive and subtle and poisonous thing called bitterness.

Just a teeny bit, just enough bitterness that I feel justified about it. Just enough bitterness that it colors my sense of humor and peppers my thoughts, but it doesn't show up on my face. Hidden so well I didn't even see it at first. I almost missed it. A slight hint of bitter, just a little on the side, for dipping in now and again.

It doesn't matter too much which things in life I've chosen to flavor this way. I haven't been a picky bitter person. But there it is. Bitterness at the desolation of life. Bitterness at people who apparently have no pain. Bitterness at women who have kids to spare. Bitterness because I lost. I lost the contest, the race, the fight.

I have been bitter at well-meaning people who see the new baby girl in my arms and say, "Oh, isn't that so amazing! It all comes full circle." Come again? They talk as if I had crashed my car and the insurance company paid for a brand-new one. Would you like it if I said that to you about husband number two? "Oh, it's not so bad now that you have a new husband. Forget about how you were cheated on and had your heart smashed to bits and were left alone in life. It's all totally cool now." Getting a new whatever it is that you lost completely makes up for it, right? Wrong. As if!

See? Bitter.

I drown in my thoughts and memories of dark days, of excruciating pain, thinking, *Is this really how my life is going down? My daughter has died, and her body is wrapped in linen and buried in a tiny pine box in the local town cemetery. And there's nothing I can do about it except curl up in the fetal position.*

Thankfully, bitterness is not the only change in me, and it's not even the most obvious or most impactful. In fact, the bitterness was just the beginning—the pothole, the roadblock to moving forward. Moving forward is where I want to go, heavenward. But we can't do that until we look honestly at our situation—the good, the bad, and the nasty. Bitterness is bad, yes, but the good? It took some searching, some scratching the surface, some deep cleaning to find it. Becoming aware of my hindering attitude of bitterness started a chain reaction that has since led to those bigger, better things—a deepening of faith, a realization that all things point to eternity; and this life, with all its troubles, is quickly coming to an end. I'm banking on this unseen eternity with my very next breath, holding on to the confidence that what I hope for will actually happen.

All I have endured and traveled through over the last six years has brought me much closer to Jesus, even while it has simultaneously flung me into the deepest crevice of loneliness and pain and confusion. It's the strangest dichotomy; this tarnished life has given me confidence and maturity and has at the same time shown me how small and foolish I can be. I'm daily trying to make sense of it all, trying to figure out how to live in grief while at the same time actually live.

We all have a story. We all have tragedies and losses and heartaches and miracles and real life, and while so much of life is glorious, sometimes it gets ugly. No one is exempt. We share in this thing called humanity, and I want us to feel—really face head-on—the reality of life with all its pimples and less attractive bits. I believe it makes the joy more vibrant, the laughter louder and stronger. So bear with me, cry with me, but please, please, laugh with me.

Three

#BLESSED

I wear glasses. Thick ones. Coke bottles, really. It's completely cringeworthy, but I confess I was rather proud of the tinted ones I had that were so popular in 1985. You know them: gigantic, squarish lenses with a line of blue tint on the top portion, then clear in the middle, then pink on the bottom portion—ever providing the glamorous look of blue eye shadow and pink blush. Yeah, superhot in an eighties kind of way. If only my permed hair would've feathered out on the sides, then the boy with the parachute pants and cropped neon yellow muscle shirt who sat in the second row would have liked me.

Anyway, I got my glasses in the fourth grade and suffered through the rest of elementary and junior high with those sweet babies, along with braces and horrible hair, until I upgraded to contact lenses in ninth grade—thank you, Jesus. My point is not my awkward years, nor is it to garner your sympathy; it's that I'm incredibly nearsighted, so much so that I often see things distortedly. Yesterday, when I saw a piece of wadded-up string that I was positive was a black widow, I quarantined the area and swooped up the baby lightning fast. Myopia can be a problem, causing a girl to scream bloody murder without good reason.

As I've walked through my season of deep grief, I have come to realize it's not only my eyes that are nearsighted but also the sight that's in my heart and mind. While drying out from being blasted with a fire hose of Bible verses and so many hurtful clichés about loss, I've become aware that I can't see past my own nose, much less my situation of suffering. So when Romans 8:28—or some other supposedly confident and cheerful verse—is spouted by some well-meaning soul, I see it distortedly.

How can everything work together for good for those called according to God's purpose? Does Paul not know my daughter suffered and died? Does he not realize people are broken and abused and betrayed? How can these things be good? Is he nuts?

It's in this gradual realization of my own obscured vision that I've come to see how so many of us in Western Christian culture have such a skewed view of God's goodness. There is a selfishness in our Christianity—in the thoughtless, consumer-driven, #blessed culture we find on the shelves of Christian bookstores. We throw around the word *blessing* haphazardly, as if God is a supernatural Santa Claus just waiting to bring treats to good little girls and boys.

But what of truly suffering believers? What about the newly homeless family who has watched helplessly while sickness settled in and took every last penny? What about the people forced to work the most disgusting jobs—in slaughterhouses, in public restrooms, in fields picking poison-covered produce—just to get by? What does our view of God and his blessings have to say to them? Have the homeless and destitute signed up for a different brand of Christianity than I? Is God's goodness the same for the middle-class, Honda-driving, well-fed, and fully insured as it is for those who are devastated and afflicted? What does *blessed* even mean?

My adult life, and particularly my married life, was quite "blessed" for the first eleven years. It was very pretty, very Instagrammable. The highs were gloriously high, and the lows weren't so low as to be deal-breakers. Not too long after we began to date, Britt and I started going to a Bible study. Two party animals by nature, we found Jesus together and were moved and transformed by God's Word. My husband was born into a surfboard-making family, owners of the top brand in the world, and he was destined to take over the business. But upon hearing a different call from Jesus just three months after we married, Britt took over the college group at our church and became ordained as a pastor, thereby ending our careers as heathens for good. Attendance at the meetings multiplied from eight kids to eight hundred. It was rocking, it was a blast, and, though we had the usual ups and downs in ministry, it was successful and amazing. The experience bred deep relationships and allowed us to witness many miracles.

Within six years we had our son, Isaiah, became pregnant with Daisy immediately after a miscarriage, and obeyed a new calling to plant a church in our hometown. Four hundred people came to the first service—and Reality, our very own church baby, was born. It was wonderful and fulfilling right off the bat. We lived in a pretty house in a charming neighborhood and neatly filled our three-bedroom, two-bathroom fortress of hardwood and wainscoting with cute kids: one boy, one girl. Our marriage was solid and satisfying, and my husband was exemplary, always working hard, rising at four a.m. and putting in thirteen-hour days while still giving us his all when he was home. We had surf dates, picnics by the lake, and fly-fishing trips to the family cabin in Montana. Blessed marriage, blessed kids, blessed house, blessed life.

Then *bam!* Right in the middle of all that pretty, cancer snuck in the side door, dropped its drawers, and made a mess all over. Caught off guard by the hovering nearness of death, the change in atmosphere turned foul. I found myself asking where all the blessing went. Why was I suddenly sprawled out on my backside, legs flayed, scratching for control like an overturned turtle? Suddenly all the blessings looked, well, cheap.

Strangely, the abrupt switch in circumstances generated a humiliating feeling. It's uncomfortable to be so vulnerable. One minute you're cruising the Pacific Coast Highway with the top down, wind gently tousling your perfectly layered hair, and the next it's raining on your leather seats, you have a flat tire, and you're waiting for the tow truck. You wrap your arms around your knees as the other cars fly by, filled with passengers safe and warm, bopping to their favorite songs while you just hope you don't get recognized.

After all my years as a Christian and living in this great country where we are stuffed to the gills with plenty, I've come to realize that *blessed* means something completely different to God than it does to us. We want it to mean that everything is perfect all the time. No speed bumps, no bruises, no pain. Not even a bad hair day. But unless I want my soul to disintegrate under the heavy hand of loss, I find that as I live another day and face another heartache, I need to open my eyes and see beyond. I need to see with sharp focus what the Bible really says about blessing, God's goodness, and living an abundant life.

You know, Jesus' disciples crack me up. They seem like my kind of people. They were working folk, sinners, a brotherhood, and—well, let's just say they were keeping it country. I love how they could be so teachable one moment, learning from the lips of the Messiah about his coming suffering, death, and resurrection—basically the most pressingly important thing—and then the next moment they were pulling Jesus aside to ask for special recognition and honor, for their definition of *blessing*.

"Sure, Jesus, that's nice. Now, back to me." (See Mark 10:33–37.)

Really, guys? Unbelievable!

But aren't we just the same? We tend to nod and say "yeah, yeah" to so many of the most important things he wants to tell us. Then, as quickly as possible, we try to refocus the conversation on "what really matters": our own wants and desires. It's easy to point the finger, to laugh out loud at Peter's foibles and James's and John's zealous and thunderous proclamations, but that is you and that is me. We are the same. We see things through an unfocused, muddied lens, not as they really are.

Jesus is so loving, so warmhearted and tender. I always imagine him gently guiding me to a better place after I've failed to see clearly: "Maybe if you feel like it, Kate, or feel led, or feel called, would you want to journal about seeing things from God's perspective, possibly looking just a teeny bit past your own? Only if that feels right to you while you're having your fair-trade coffee and gluten-free croissant. And yes, I'll be your boyfriend and hold your hand and affirm your musings while you fill the pages of leather journals with the incredibly important feelings from your heart."

Or sometimes, I imagine him good-naturedly shaking his shoulder-length, naturally highlighted hair, thinking, *Aren't they cute? Aw, they'll learn. Just kids.* Then he picks us up and swings us around, never wrinkling or spoiling his white robe and light blue sash.

But as I've dug more deeply into Scripture, I've found it to be a different story. In Matthew 16:21–23, Jesus again predicted his death and resurrection to the disciples. Peter took Jesus aside (first red flag—I mean, who takes Jesus aside?) and reprimanded him (what?!), saying, "No way! Heaven forbid that this should happen." Peter was filtering the terrifying but lifesaving words of Jesus through his own lens—his finite, natural, man lens. Can't say that I blame him, by the way. It would also seem to me that the torture and murder of the Son of Man would be the most deplorable of things to happen; but the well-intentioned Peter was about to get the smackdown from the gentle Lamb of God.

"Get away from me, Satan!" Jesus said. "You are seeing things merely from a human point of view, not from God's" (v. 23).

Um, did Jesus just call Peter "Satan"? It seems that my imaginary pushover Jesus is just that: *imaginary.* This was no wink of the eye, no waving away of errant thinking, but a solid rebuke. I mean, getting called a jerk is a bummer, and liar or thief or tramp is never good. But Satan?

Jesus meant business. He was about to do the hardest

thing in the history of the universe, to embrace pain and suffering and hardship, and he didn't need any of his buddies tempting him to do otherwise.

Just like Peter, we flinch at the slightest prospect of discomfort. We've been conditioned to expect ease as a sign of God's blessing, but that is not how Jesus would have us live. It's not how he lived. The last time I checked, he came to give life—abundant life—but maybe that looks a little different from what we thought.

I need this new vision; I need this rebuke. I still find myself momentarily lost in memories driven mercilessly by my darkest moments, when my tongue is thick in my mouth as if numbed by novocaine and my heart is lodged firmly in my throat. I relive the long nights at the hospital in flashes, the burning sensation of fear taking over my skin. My eyes prickle, face hot, when I think of Daisy's sunken eyes, her weak body, her inability to lift her head. And I feel the emptiness in my body caused by the moment when her lifeless shell was taken from my arms and left them hanging like an old rusty swing, nodding in the breeze to no one in particular. That is my life.

And it feels anything but blessed.

I think the core of how we define *blessing*, is how we feel the love of God—tangibly with the way our lives shake out, with what we receive. If life goes well for me, then I am blessed. God must love me. But if things don't go according to plan, suddenly I am thrown for a loop.

Doesn't God promise to care for us? Isn't his love shown most clearly when he blesses his children with good things?

In Jesus' Sermon on the Mount, he tells us not to worry, convinces us we are far more valuable than the birds God provides for, lacking nothing. He promises that if God cares so wonderfully for the wildflowers, he will certainly care for us. And by the way, why do we have so little faith?

I'll tell you why: because Daisy died. My daughter endured brutal sickness and died a tragic death. Because God allowed so much tragedy in my family. Because it appeared he didn't hear our cries, because he turned his face from our deepest desire. Because my sparrow fell, and he didn't seem to notice. That's why I have so little faith. That's why it's difficult to believe I am valuable to God.

But here's where I'm wrong. Here's where I have exchanged what I see dimly for what God is crystal clear about. Here's where I shake up our Western understanding of blessing. Whether we are aware of it or not, we tie God's love directly to the tangible presence of what we consider to be good things, but what if his care for us means something else entirely? What if my life turning out exactly the way I wanted it to doesn't equal God loving me? I didn't feel God's love for a while in my grief, but it was there. I had just forgotten the truth.

Remember how I was so irked by Paul and his "all things work together" spiel? I was so busy asking Paul snarky questions that I missed how he himself had a tough row to hoe. Mere days after his conversion on the road to Damascus, he started receiving death threats. In the coming years, he was beaten with rods, whipped, given thirty-nine lashes five different times, imprisoned, shipwrecked, stoned. He knew hunger, thirst, heat, and cold, faced dangers in cities, deserts, and on seas. Paul knew suffering.

Yet he wrote this in Romans 8:35, 38–39 (emphasis mine):

> Can anything ever separate us from Christ's love? *Does it mean he no longer loves us* if we have trouble or calamity, or are persecuted, or hungry, or destitute, or in danger, or threatened with death? . . . I am convinced that nothing can ever separate us from God's love. Neither death nor life, neither angels nor demons, neither our fears for today nor our worries about tomorrow—not even the powers of hell can separate us from God's love. No power in the sky above or in the earth below—indeed, nothing in all creation will ever be able to separate us from the love of God that is revealed in Christ Jesus our Lord.

Exhale . . . The love of God is outside of circumstances. I had believed a lie.

Most of the American church believes this lie. Blessing does not mean we get our life dished out on a silver platter. No, it means that while we were enemies of God, he loved us. Lose sight of that love, and we miss out on a whole world of real life. When we hang on to false ideologies, it kills our joy. It makes us stoop down to whatever the current state of affairs is, rather than stand tall in the confidence of one who is secure in love.

But when we humble ourselves and ask God to show us the truth, we will find that after the initial sting of seeing our shortcomings comes the sweet release of repentance. Peter knew firsthand those precious words: "Repent . . . that times of refreshing may come" (Acts 3:19 NIV). And so, I have found myself waking up like the blooming coral sunrise peeking through the canyon where I live.

It does not happen overnight; these things take time. Even just last night I sat on my patio, watching the sun burn and sizzle lazily down behind the horses in the pasture, quenched by the ocean beyond the hill. As I watched the stars timidly tiptoeing out one by one, I felt bare before the Creator. Bats flitted around the stark silhouette of the eucalyptus trees, the crescent moon hung delicately in translucent lavender and indigo, and I remembered yet again that he sees things not as I do. I am so small. I am one of seven billion, and yet he knows my name, knows my hurt, knows my future. Wrapped in the same creamy white, downy blanket that I often wrapped around my sick Daisy, I just sat. Prayed. Repented. And let the truth of his love wash over my tired soul.

I needed, and I need, time alone with him. I needed, and I need, to look up. We all need to look up. Please, for the love of your Maker, look up. Look up from the screen, the chores, the distractions, the things that make us believe we're less than blessed. Look up from the unnecessary things we cram into our lives, the things we tightly wedge in every corner to keep us full. Give God a chance to speak; allow yourself to be alone with him, creating space to see the way he is loving you beyond your human understanding.

It takes courage; it takes honesty. It takes willingness to be convicted, to repent, and to be healed. It takes willingness to be softened, willingness to face your demons. It takes guts. But that's where the healing begins, in the counterintuitive place of surrender and in that place of perspective.

It's time to see things not from our human point of view but from God's and to let Jesus call us out. We need to know how to navigate the open wounds and the unmet heart desires of this risky and dangerous life, but we have not been left in those hard and confusing places on our own. We are free to thrash and mourn and be human in our heartbreak, but when it's time to set the anguish aside, there is a way out of the pit of despair. We have the key, the map. We have the correct lens prescription. We are the recipients of ancient mysteries privy only to the friends of God.

I'm not sure if Jesus would say, "Get behind me,

Satan," to my blindness, but I do know that he desires us to be on the same page. True fellowship begins here. Like with a bestie or a spouse, the more we exchange ideas and truths and show who we really are, the more deeply we will come to know God's love. I've found that the more I press into this, the more I don't hinge God's blessing and love upon my circumstances. And that sparks hope.

So I dialogue with God, I read his Word, I listen to his voice. I crowd closer to him so that I can hear more clearly, so that I can understand more fully. This purposeful re-arrangement of my point of view has given me wings. My faith has always been there, but the way I see things has changed; it has aged, matured, cured to a fuller and more developed flavor. Instead of reactive living according to circumstances, I have learned to peel back a few layers, to see what the heartbeat behind this crazy life is all about. I am discovering the way Jesus seeps from tears of sorrow and joy alike. I am finding security in his undeniable love, and it makes my heart sing.

Let's shift our thinking from merely human to divine. Let's trade in our Coke-bottle glasses for the lenses of truth. Let's adjust our definitions of *blessings* and *hardship*, to live abundantly and purposefully, even walking through the valley of the shadow of death. This life isn't all just a beach, but that doesn't mean it isn't blessed.

Wind rushed fresh in my face, and my hair flapped behind me like a carefree kite tail. With the sun on my shoulders, I leaned forward into the experience. Then I heard from a car window: "Nice ride!"

It came from a wizened old woman in the middle of the Trader Joe's parking lot. I had hopped on the back of my cart right out of the gate, careening straight toward my Honda Pilot, and I was booking it. Smiling to myself at her encouragement, I rode that thing like the wind all the way through the parking lot then filled my trunk full with food God had provided, whispering prayers of thanks.

I had gotten used to going to the grocery store wearing a baseball cap and sunglasses. Head down and feet dragging, hoping not to make eye contact with anyone. But now times of refreshing had begun to come. Understanding God's love outside of circumstances sparked a flicker of light, a brightness that comes with the readjustment of perspective. A freedom that makes a girl feel loved, even while she grieves.

I can feel the atmosphere beginning to change again. This time from the stifling covering of gloom to one steadily giving way to joy. I can feel the emotional cloud cover beginning to burn off as the sun shines more brightly. To practice enjoying the sweetness of life is a wondrous thing. I think I'm off to a great start.

Four

CRAZY MESSY

Everyone has a story. Some stories beam bright and pretty but secretly hide darkness that is yet to be revealed. Others are openly dredged in sorrow and make you cringe at first glance, but then the light shines through so brilliantly that there is no mistaking something wonderful lies underneath it all. Stories teach, whether the heroine is unshakable or the protagonist is a blind fool, whether the outcome is comedy or tragedy. We learn from others' experiences. There is precious value in sharing and hearing the stories of our lives, extraordinary importance in the laying bare of the soul.

God has met me through story. He has introduced me to the reality of life on earth and the goodness of Jesus through the stories of other women's lives. Women of Scripture who appear to have it all, or who have enormous reputations for godliness, or even women who have sullied reputations. He has invited me to investigate open-mindedly, to shed my preconceived notions and my prejudices against these ancient ladies.

It's as if he said, "Kate, I want you to meet some people. You have more in common with them than you realize, so why don't you head down to the beach and hang for a bit? Get your bronze on and go deep."

And so, I've enjoyed getting to know these powerful women of the Bible a bit better. I've enjoyed spending time with them while lying in the sand, Ray-Bans reflecting the sparkling Pacific. Together we have spilled our guts, so to speak. With them I have found solidarity, encouragement, sympathy, and rebuke. Thank you, God, for introducing me to true grit.

The Bible is full of women I look forward to being friends with in heaven, as well as a few I can live without. (Jezebel, anybody?) One woman in particular fits both categories. Almost all of you know her, and you're either on her team or you want to kick her to the curb. She's the perfect woman, the pinnacle of femininity and strength, the zenith of amazing. You know who I'm talking about. You can find her in Proverbs 31. There she is, perched in all her literary glory, all any woman can be and do wrapped up in twenty-one little no-pressure verses—the unattainable, overly long list of what makes a woman excellent.

Right now I'm sure many of you are bristling at the very mention of this passage of Scripture. Give me a second and let me try and win you over. We all need biblical instruction. We live in a wishy-washy culture shaken and stirred by loud voices selling opposing versions of what it means to be a woman. Meanwhile we carry the baggage acquired from personal experience and navigating the truckloads of Christian books written about what a godly girl should be. We have found ourselves in a confused whirlwind state on the topic of femininity, which has got to stop. I'm convinced it's not as complicated as we have been led to believe.

I'm asking you now to walk away from any notions that have been stewing around in your heart and mind since you got your first period and realized there was no going back on this womanhood thing. Set down the movies, books, well-meaning church ladies and aunties, pop stars and nuns, and pick up your Bible. Bring on the pure Word of God, not another person's interpretation. Don't be stuffed in a box made by human hands or be burdened by another era's or individual's version of femininity's rules.

Let's check it out for ourselves with fresh eyes and give this girl another look. Admittedly, Proverbs 31's description of the ultimate woman feels both aspirational and completely unrealistic at first. She works hard, she brings in cash, she has foresight and intelligence, she's generous, she has a great reputation, she's creative and industrious, and her Etsy shop is going off. She even wears beautiful clothing she has made herself. She's so cool . . . but she's also the girl we love to hate!

She's like all the pins in your Pinterest account. She's the hairdo you're itching to try, or the picture of the girl whose yoga pants make her butt look so good it brings inspiration to your "workout" board. She's the salads and smoothies you want to make with all the produce from your local organic farm, or maybe the maple bacon cupcakes or gourmet vegan doughnuts, or whatever you're into. This mystery Proverbs 31 woman is the ultimate Pinterest pin for awesomeness. Strength, dignity, bravery, trust, creativity, ingenuity, kindness—she's legit. I have mad respect for her and all, but, honestly, she bugs me with all that amazingness.

My husband, who knows me better than I know myself, has gently informed me that I'm defensive when it comes to correction or any type of conflict. (No, I'm not!) I can't stand the thought of not being awesome, and naturally awesome at that—the very inventor of awesome. I want to be an awesome wife, an awesome mom, an awesome daughter, an awesome friend, an awesome Christian, an awesome person. Yet when you stand me next to the biblical paragon of female awesome, well . . . let's just say it's why we don't want to hang out with the bride too long at a wedding. Radiant beauty makes everything around it appear shabby. Thanks, Proverbs 31 woman, for making the rest of us look bad. I'm sure you didn't mean to.

I know every single one of us fears or at least is aware of others' opinions. It's not just me. None of us wants to expose our own mangy selves to the watching world.

We post pictures of carefully made-up faces, body shots taken at angles most flattering. We show off our party decor, our brightest days, our Sunday best. Fabulous is the new normal.

I've historically gone with the opposite strategy; I don't want anyone to think I'm someone I'm not. I tend to take extreme measures to ensure people get what they see, because I don't want to disappoint people down the road as they get to know the real me. I've even gone so far as to behave like a cavewoman on the first date with my now-husband.

I've always been a girl who could pack it away. I like food, and when you've spent the day surfing and running around on the beach, you can work up a fierce hunger. So, at dinner that first night, I ordered whatever sounded good to my growling stomach—unlike the modus operandi of women in America, who prefer to appear dainty and order "just a small salad, I'm really not that hungry." Liars. A whole country of single women lying to potential suitors.

Not me. I decided I didn't want this guy to realize one day that I wasn't who he signed up for, so I went for it. We sat there, and I slurped and gulped and relished and licked the bowl. Okay, I didn't lick the bowl in a public place, but I've got no shame at home. Meantime, he sat across from me, having ordered a small plate of lasagna. He wiped his mouth in between bites like a gentleman. So cute.

Later, when he brought me home to have dinner with his parents, I again opted for my usual portion: piled high. His mom is a great cook, and I was nineteen with the metabolism of, well, a nineteen-year-old who is superactive. Again, I enjoyed every bite. We had a lovely dinner. I charmed Britt's dad with a comment about how he looks just like Eric Clapton then later said good-bye while blithely leaning against my powder-blue '71 VW Squareback. I wore Doc Martens, thrift store 501s for men, a maroon mock turtleneck bodysuit, and a bomber jacket. Superhot in a nineties kind of way. What I found out later was that after I left, when Britt asked his parents what they thought about me, his dad said, in his deep, contemplative voice, "Well, son, you should be careful about a girl who eats more than you do."

So much for attempting to avoid letting others down. As a side note, I have since entered the twenty-first century and cleaned up my manners, but I still tend to be very transparent—whether I'm meeting someone for the first time (what would you like to know about my checkered past?), speaking from a pulpit (I have been known to talk freely about regrettably embarrassing things), or with old and dear friends (lamenting formerly perky body parts, anyone?). No surprises here, people.

But hey, before we succumb to our own puny issues, before we hate on our P31 girl for making the rest of us look bad, let's just remember that she wasn't an actual person! She was a description of the ultimate woman given by a wise mama to her kingly son.

I'm sure, when the time comes for my son to marry, I'll encourage him to shoot for the best. He is my son, after all . . . I would do anything for that kid. No really, anything. Like, I'd scratch the eyes out of any girl who would break his heart or treat him badly. I mean it. And I'm sure this queen wouldn't think twice before putting a fair maiden who wasn't fit for her prince in a headlock.

So when we read about P31 girl and her awesomeness, let's not berate ourselves because we don't measure up. Let's be grateful we have a good model. We learn by example, and if we didn't have stellar examples to aspire to, we would likely aim for mediocre. So even though this model woman sounds annoyingly unrealistic, you know what they say: shoot for the moon, and even if you miss, you'll land among the stars.

Take a look at this passage again, freeing yourself from cultural implications. Set aside your personal preferences and experiences, and you will be inspired by the strength, the creativity, the honor, and the wisdom and purpose this woman possesses. Go ahead. Read it. I think you'll be pleasantly surprised.

When I read this passage with an open heart, what I really home in on, what helps me not get hung up on all the ways we fall short, is verse 25: "She is clothed with strength and dignity, and she laughs without fear of the future."

Laughing without fear. I have such longing to be in a place in life where I can indulge in this seemingly simple activity, this innocent and lovely thing. I absolutely love to laugh. Until 2009 I would say it was a defining characteristic of my whole life. I've been known to laugh at inappropriate times—such as, but not limited to, funerals (story coming) and weddings (I once had to crawl under the table because I could not stop crying/laughing). I was raised to have the most fun humanly possible, to surf my guts out and dance at weddings, to giggle for sport.

But the reality is, the recent years have been about crying. Shedding tears is such a frequent occurrence that it has become part of my identity. Sorrow has cut deeply into my previous life's goal of carefree fun.

I know it's true for some of you too. Some of us are identified by tears of tragedy and some by tears of sin. Life is harsh. We walk around with scarlet letters on our chests. Mine is posted large and loud for my small town to see—the glaring *B* for bereavement. Others bear the quintessential *A* for adultery or the *I* for infertility. Perhaps some have a blazing *S* for substance abuse or the excruciatingly prevalent *D* for divorce. We the broken are easily identifiable.

We haven't all been the Proverbs 31 woman. She's not even on the radar for some. Most of us can't say our choices have been so good, so godly, that we have no fear of them bringing anything other than blessing.

I would bet each one of us has made a few messes in our lives. I have. The effects linger and begin to show up on our countenances—lines and blemishes that weren't there before. It's a very real thing to read about this fictitiously flawless woman and think, *I'm not her. In fact, my choices stink, and my life shows it. I wouldn't even know where to start, how to scrub clean and bandage the wounds enough to get to the business of godliness.* Sometimes it's tempting to throw in the towel and give in to darkness, give in to foolishness, and give up.

But even when we do all we can to meticulously make the right choices, to fill our charts with gold stars, the poop still hits the fan. Loyal spouses suffer betrayal, healthy people become debilitated in accidents that weren't their fault, talented and hardworking people lose their jobs when the company sells . . . Even moms who do everything they can for their sick little girls end up with their hearts broken. Without warning we can lose the very things we grasped with every ounce of strength. It seems, sometimes, that this life is far out of our control.

Maybe even most of the time, it's difficult to believe God's goodness to us. All the felicitous promises from the Bible fall on deaf ears, only to bounce off and roll under the couch, lost among the dust bunnies and missing puzzle pieces. Who can actually laugh when life is so cruel? Apparently not someone who has lived any real life.

I'm tempted to think of the writer of Proverbs 31 as

a girl who was naïve, silly, and inexperienced in reality. Come on—who on earth writes this stuff? Who was this bright-eyed and bushy-tailed champion of holiness and optimism? Let's just say the answer to these irascible questions is a tad unexpected.

Many Bible commentators agree that the writer of the last chapter of Proverbs was most likely Bathsheba. Remember her? You know that girl. What's she famous for? Bathing on the roof of her house. Yeah, I totally have the visual too. Beautiful spring day, long luscious locks, pre-baby body. That's probably how most of us remember her. The girl whose beauty and nudity enticed a handsome king to warm his bed for a night. Not the best of first impressions.

We can make our judgments about her and call her all sorts of colorful names, but the bottom line is—the 2 Samuel account does not tell us whether she was showing off or attempting to do her thing modestly. I'm not gonna lie; it does sound sketchy. I mean, in my imagination she was running water through her hair, head tipped back like a risqué shampoo commercial, not so much scrubbing her armpits.

Did she have a servant holding up a sheet, or was she secretly pleased to be watched by a handsome king? We don't know. What she was doing was bathing in the *mikveh*, performing the ritual cleansing bath Jewish women take when they are finished with their monthly period. It signified that she was purified and ready for her husband after two weeks of abstinence. So on the day Bathsheba was beckoned by the king, she was supposed to have been home making babies with Uriah—her strapping soldier husband—but he was away at war.

The Bible is silent as to whether or not Bathsheba welcomed an adulterous relationship with David, but the more I get to know Bathsheba, my guess is his advance was scary and unwanted. Chances are she didn't have much of a choice. After the whole sordid experience, she undoubtedly felt heavy under the weight of sin, having been used by the king for a night of pleasure and then forgotten. I'm casting my vote in favor of Bathsheba's integrity, but if I find out one day in heaven that she was just as much at fault as David, well . . . none of us is better than she. Most of us have made some pretty heinous mistakes. I've decided I love her regardless of blame and admire the woman she became, which is the whole reason we are even talking about her.

Apparently, after the infamous escapade, her pregnancy was the only reason that Bathsheba's involvement with David went any further. Enough time had gone by for her to realize the consequence of their illicit union, and she sent word of her pregnancy to the king by way of a note. Can you imagine? I mean, what do you say to the dude who made you his booty call, got you pregnant while your husband was out risking his neck for the kingdom, and then went on his merry way?

Did she want to pour out her heart, claim his love? Did she want to let him know this was not her usual, that she was not that kind of girl? Did she want to cuss him out? Were there tear stains on the note? Perfume? Was it folded carefully in the shape of those notes we passed in high school? Or was she worried the messenger would read it and feel the need to divulge the most iniquitous secret she held? It seemed her very fate was sealed up in that little message, that terse note that said simply "I'm pregnant."

Bathsheba's husband, Uriah, is described as one of David's "mighty men." He had been out fighting that spring with the rest of the Israelite army, so there was no valid excuse for the origin of her growing child. I can imagine the terror Bathsheba felt, the sickening guilt, the desire for cleanliness. I imagine she felt like a trapped animal, caged and awaiting a formidable master. Trembling at the consequences of a sin that would soon become obvious, that would make her an outcast worthy of the death penalty.

But the Lord knew. He knew there was more for this precious woman than being used for a one-night stand, more in store for her than a lifetime of regret and fear and hunger and shame. He had more life for her to experience: highs and lows, joys and sorrows, and a calling marked by dignity and wisdom. There was forgiveness and more heartache to come, but most of all there was a chance in the future to bring God glory. A chance to encourage women over the millennia and a chance to walk again,

her head held high with the beauty of strength and wisdom and purpose.

We don't know everything about Bathsheba, but we
do know for sure that she had much to cry about. She was
not only scandalously used by the king and illegitimately
pregnant, but her husband Uriah—who apparently was a
great guy, serving his country and refusing to flake out on
his men even when David offered him leave to come home
and sleep with Bathsheba—was murdered by David to
cover up his sin. The baby boy she conceived with David
died soon after he was born, and Bathsheba became one
of David's many wives. She was taken from a good life
with a good man to live a lonely life among many other
women who were used and kept like property. Pretty sure
I'd hate to live in a harem that shared a husband, regardless of all the free swag.

God eventually comforted Bathsheba's numerous
losses with a son: Solomon. Someone to love and care
for, someone to share closeness and affection, someone
to raise up and encourage. Years later when he became
a grown man and king, his loving mother wrote words
of wisdom to him. And so we have the last chapter of
Proverbs, in which she described the internationally
famous, worthy woman of nobility and kindness.

Bathsheba didn't have a perfect life free of sin and
bummers and tragedy. Despite being a wife of the king,
she did not live on easy street. But she grew up. She

became the mother of the future king, and something stirred in her that said, *Look, this is what is good. This is where you want to be; this is what's wise and beautiful and full of honor.* She had seen pain and sin and betrayal firsthand and suffered consequences out of her control. She had felt the devastation of love and death and despair. She had mourned the murder of her husband and the loss of her infant son. The woman had some street cred, which changes everything for me when I read her words to Solomon, her description of an excellent woman.

No longer do I balk at these lofty verses. No longer do I desire to throw them out, assuming that the writer was judgmental, legalistic, and riding a high horse. Instead, I accept them, respect them, and desire to live them out. The woman behind them was real, broken, and had risen above.

Real-life stories bring salve to a wounded soul. Knowing Bathsheba and I share in some sad experiences draws me deep into her life, and seeing her rise from the ashes buoys my confidence in God's goodness—that I, too, will survive the great loss.

I stumbled upon Bathsheba in the months following Daisy's death, after the laziness subsided and the bitterness began to settle. It was a kind of grief support group; we shared stories, compared lots. Like when you get a sponsor to see you through the hardest months of healing from addiction, she was there for me. When I was the only woman I knew who had experienced death so close to my heart, I remembered how she had too. In the quiet hours of a house bereft of the shouts and footsteps of a child, she whispered strength, dignity, and fearlessness. When I was comforted with a pregnancy, I remembered she had been too. She showed me how to be loyal to another child while grieving the first. She held my hand in the gloom, leaned close to my ear, and whispered, "Me too."

On the days that I felt publicly conspicuous, the unfortunate *B* emblazoned upon me, she walked beside me wearing the same letter. I was not alone. I started to look up, to see and understand that there is life beyond the hurt. I felt some of the heaviness lifting at the very thought of sharing in such hardship.

Because I had a friend in Bathsheba, because of her story, I could count on her example. The first few times that I had opportunity to laugh during those early days of mourning, it felt foreign. It felt wrong, sacrilegious, amiss. But I had seen her mourn, I had read her story of strength, and I had experienced the reality of her loneliness and shame. I knew that she would one day tell her son that an excellent woman laughs without fear of the future—not because she is perfect or her life is perfect, but because it is good and right and honors God. So began my freedom to giggle, my freedom to reclaim the goodness of the life God had given me. A beginning that opened up the way to healing.

Perhaps my favorite thing about Bathsheba and

Proverbs 31 is that after her crazy messy life she can tell you that the future is worth smiling about. Dignity and strength are beautiful, and kindness wins over manipulation and harshness. The Holy Spirit through Bathsheba is worth listening to, I think. I want to breathe the air she breathes, laugh the way she laughs. I want to say with all confidence that I, like Bathsheba, can come through some of life's most brutal beatings and still be kind, still be strong, still laugh without fear.

Five

NO, YOU DID LAUGH

The finest snippets of life are those in which laughter is at the core—events meaningful enough to be etched into our brains. Such times bring deep healing and shape who we become. They're the kind we frame and display in a place of prominence, the ones we bring up around campfires for years to come, reliving the hilarity and the rapture.

Once in a while laughter simply overcomes you, coming from deep in your belly, the sound filled with joy and hope and enduring love. One of those times that I will never forget was the spring of 1997, when I was twenty-two years old. I had just gotten off work at Channel Islands, which I loved so much—the surf shop belonging to my then-boyfriend's (now-husband's) parents. It had been a long, hot day of folding T-shirts, hanging bikinis, making cute displays, and chatting up all the locals. Surf shops tend to be something of a hub for people who share a love for the greatest sport on earth. No, I'm not biased.

My boyfriend had called me on the landline at work and asked me to come down to the beach to watch the sunset with him. Sweet, but not entirely the usual. Our evenings normally consisted of surfing then gorging on burritos and ice cream. But no matter, it sounded fun! So I went.

On the beach we held hands, we chatted, he chased me around with a dead jellyfish on a stick, and we were caught up in the bliss belonging to two young people who didn't have a whole lot of life under their belts yet. Unaware of what the future would bring, we were completely in the moment. We got to where the waves began to break, and he suggested we sit down in the sand.

At the moment the sun sank below the horizon, he turned to me and said, "Katie, you know I love you, and I want you to be my girl. Will you marry me?" Oh, my heart. I knew something was up his sleeve! That's when it happened.

The laughter began deep in my belly and bubbled out of me. It spilled over my lips and down the front of my shirt and all over the sand. It flowed so freely, as if there were an endless supply of joyful noise all bound up inside me. More and more and more came, and soon tears came with it—giving motion and texture to the joy, the abandon of relishing in another's love, the realization that someone wanted to give me his name, give me a home, give me a diamond ring to seal the whole delicious deal.

I laughed so much, so thoroughly, that my soon-to-be fiancé confusedly asked, "So? Will you?" I loudly proclaimed, "Yes! A thousand yeses!" No joke. If you need to throw up, do it now. But I loved it, every second of it. The pure laughter of freedom and love and happiness and the anticipation of more good to come. Sigh.

Then there are other times, when laughter seems completely inappropriate. I was at the funeral of a dear woman from our church about eight or nine months after Daisy died. She was a wonderful woman, very loved, a feisty little thing with a great sense of humor, which is why I don't feel so bad about what comes next. During the service one of her daughters spoke about how being a mom sometimes requires doing the difficult thing. She shared a story about how excruciating it was to give her own young daughter painful treatments for leukemia, then linked the idea to a time when her mother had helped her off a ski lift the hard way in order to save her from further danger.

Right at that moment, my husband leaned over and whispered into my ear, "Thanks a lot, Mom, for shoving me off the lift." I was struck with the funny stick so hard, there was no hope. I yukked and yukked with shoulders shaking and tears streaming, all the while praying to remain unnoticed—which is virtually impossible in a setting like that. I hid my head in my husband's shoulder while we both had an absolute letdown of emotion in the form of uncontrollable laughter.

Apparently we hid this fact well. A close friend of mine brought over a box of tissues, thinking the leukemia thing was dredging up grim thoughts from our own daughter's treatment. Honestly, that had passed me right by, and I believe God allowed us to find humor in an impossible situation for the good of our hearts.

By the way—super sorry, dear deceased friend, for cracking up at your funeral. And to any friends who were at the same funeral and are just now discovering the truth about my "breakdown"? Well, I hope you still love me. Survival mode, y'all.

Laughter is the strangest thing. It can be healing, literally. It can inject an impossibly terrible situation with a whoosh of fresh air. Sharing laughter fosters a bond between humans. In its purest form it brings life. When a baby laughs, it's like no other sound. I'm sure 99 percent of you have watched the YouTube video of all those babies strewn over their sweet mama, laughing simultaneously. Put that on repeat, please.

I even pay money to laugh. (Thank you, Tim Hawkins, for getting me through cancer, my firstborn's puberty, and having a toddler at age forty—I own all your DVDs.) Sometimes laughter seems inappropriate, but it is the only thing that can get you through a rough patch. Many times I found myself making jokes about vomit and edema in the hospital with seven-year-old Daisy. Pranking the nurses and doctors became the highlight of some pretty miserable days. I mean, what else are you going to do? I'm convinced laughter is key to survival.

I've laughed a lot in my life, lots of happy and free laughter, throwing my head back and busting a gut. But as the years have gone by and I've experienced more tough times, the lighthearted atmosphere has shifted. I have seen myself spewing a different kind of laughter: a bitter, hard-ened laughter, like a waste product of a sick heart. And it's ugly. It came poking its head out when I was unaware it was even there. Like termites hidden in wood that was once healthy.

For the past six years I've dwelt in ashes, the acrid smoke of desolation all around, and in dark times of reflection I have seen myself mocking the very idea of find-ing joy through all the sorrow. Bitter laughter has been sneaky, has hidden itself, and like spiderwebs appearing stealthily in the corners of your closet, it has come to inhabit the corners of my heart. Slowly but surely, this fractious and unwelcome guest has settled down deep. It caught me by surprise and threatened to become a way of life for me—one of cynical unbelief in God's goodness, of rancor at the horrors I've suffered.

Sometimes seeing ourselves clearly in the mirror is a bummer experience. If the last time you looked in the mirror your makeup was fresh and your hair was rock-ing, you feel pretty good about yourself. But if the reality is that you looked like a raccoon and had cilantro in your teeth, well then, you have a problem. And it takes either a close-up mirror or a true friend to let you know when there's a bat in the cave (girlfriend's code for "check your nose").

Recently I got a little spiritual mirror check. At first glance, I was generally doing pretty well—cruising right along, loving Jesus, raising babies. My faith in God, for the most part, hadn't wavered; I still worshipped with a sincere heart and desire to hear him speak. But the barely there niggling feelings of bitterness had lingered in my subconscious. Little grudges had formed, jokes indulgently made only to myself. I had thrown away joy because of something I didn't understand, because the answer to my most fervent prayer was a heavy, unalterable, ghastly no.

I realized I was living life with the limp of one who has been injured but not correctly healed. All my nasty, grievous attitudes were feeding the bitter beast in me, and it manifested itself in snappish humor. I took everything personally, was easily offended, and used dry humor as my shield.

Every time I received "comfort" that turned out to be hurtful, it fed the secret monster just a bit, the monster that hid behind a veil of wisecracks. When my temper flared at other women who complained about their children, I made jealous jokes. My conversations at home often turned snarky, bringing morale a few notches down, allowing my beastly burden to swell. My husband wondered aloud where his wife had gone, and God began to show me the truth. I was playing the victim—the very thing I can't stand in others—and I had been blind to it all along. Sin always looks better on us than on everyone else.

Slowly, gently, I awakened to this repulsive and

sinister thing growing inside me. The mocking laughter, the defense mechanism, the vice for dealing with life. I thought, *If I don't believe God's goodness for me personally, then I can't be disappointed in him. If I don't ask him for anything, then he can't slam the door in my face again.* It's almost as if I was trying to save face, but whose face was I trying to save? That's a question between me and the Creator, one that requires surrender and the flaying open of the heart. Give me some time on that one.

But God. Two of the greatest words. In Ephesians 2:4–5 (ESV), we are given the beautiful words of the good news: "But God, being rich in mercy, because of the great love with which he loved us . . . made us alive together with Christ."

But God has not seen fit to let me wallow in my sadness.

But God has been bringing my darkness into the light.

But God has not been quiet to me, even after all the hidden places, the flippant jokes about my rotten lot in life.

But God has been generously offering to trade my sorrow for gladness, my confusion for peace.

God is gently, lovingly teaching me about laughter, about himself, about life and death and goodness and pain and the future. He's giving me ways to walk in peace, to be rid of bitterness, to be strengthened. Ways that have carried me through murky times and changed my days.

He's using human experience and biblical women to show me truth in a new light, and it makes me want to laugh, makes me feel loved all over again. It reminds me that he is caring for my soul, and he is inviting me into deeper relationship.

I love reading about women in ages past—what they were like and what they did—and it's funny because nothing is new under the sun. Women will always be women. Like Miriam, we sing and dance. We throw girls-only parties like Vashti, laugh too loudly like Elizabeth, and love perfume like Mary of Bethany. We favor the dramatic and the beautiful and, like Esther, we are stronger than we let on.

But of all the extraordinary women in the Bible, I find Sarah, wife of Abraham, to be the most unpredictably relatable. Sarah, an extolled woman of faith and example to Jews and Christians throughout millennia. On the surface, she had it all. She was beautiful, married to a rich and godly man, and even had servants. She bravely obeyed God's will for her life and traveled to a foreign but promised land, and I just know she was covered in swanky accessories while she did it. She was living the dream, and it sounds sexy!

But take a closer look, and you'll see she was also a

NO, YOU DID LAUGH

woman who experienced much disappointment. Her perfect veneer of beauty and travel and wealth was just that: a veneer. It concealed her heartbreak neatly beneath the surface. Dig a little deeper, and we find out she suffered a lifetime of infertility—which was a very big deal in ancient Middle Eastern culture, when a woman's ability to have children, and scads of them, dictated her worth.

Her heart's desire was to have her empty arms filled, to lay love on a child, to nurse and nurture and raise up a tiny human she could call her own. Year after year went by, desolate and dry. I know what it is to ache to hold the small one you love, to have that reality unfulfilled, unreachable. The feminine heart thirsts for intimacy, and the motherly soul longs to provide nourishment, attention, affection, life.

Yet Sarah, this exotic and noble woman, hid deep in her heart a hope for the future. You see, God had promised to make Abraham the father of a great nation. So Sarah waited and waited for God to make good, but the years went by and she grew very old and quite discouraged. I'm sure she was ready to throw in the towel on the whole "follow God to Canaan" and "you'll be the mother of a great nation" thing.

Sometime around Genesis 16, when Sarah was in her seventies, she tried to take matters into her own hands and manipulate the situation. (I've *never* done that.) Desperate times call for desperate measures. So, out of desperation, she gave her Egyptian servant Hagar to her husband in hopes of having a baby by proxy. Let's read Genesis 16:2:

> So Sarai said to Abram, "The LORD has prevented me from having children. Go and sleep with my servant. Perhaps I can have children through her." And Abram agreed with Sarai's proposal.

Really, dude? Abe, it seems like it didn't take you very long to make the decision. Just sayin'.

Can you imagine lending your husband out for the night to your maidservant? I mean, what do you say to them? "Good luck, guys!" Or "Please go to the farthest tent down!" Or maybe you just plug your ears and say, "*Lalalalalalalala!*" Those were different days.

Then when Hagar became pregnant, her relationship with Sarah turned sketchy—surprise, surprise!—and there was contempt and fighting. Aside from the fact that God had promised Sarah, not Hagar, that she would be the mother of nations and even kings of nations, not much good could come from finding an "easy" fix, from manipulation. We cannot bend and twist God's Word to suit our desires. No matter how badly we thirst, it's never a good idea. The rift in Sarah and Hagar's relationship was immediate proof.

But we can't judge her for this, can we? Raise your

hand if you've tried to "help" God along, if you've ever been so single-minded that all else went out of focus. If you've mowed over other people in a scramble to see God's promise come to fruition. We are all so much like Sarah, yearning for our hearts' desire—hoping, believing, waiting, and getting frustrated with God's timing and trying to fix the situation on our own. Sarah's world became filled with tension, hostility, and sadness, and it was all because she took matters into her own hands.

More years went by after this epic fail, and when Sarah was ninety years old, she was again reminded of God's promise. This brings us to the event I want us to camp out on.

Picture an arid, Middle Eastern landscape, date palms burgeoning with fruit in the distance, sun smoldering in a pale sky, donkeys mournfully braying in the heat of the day. Dudes in long robes with copious amounts of facial hair, camels bearing brightly colored blankets and trinkets jangling and swinging in time with their unhurried stride. Inside the sun-bleached tent are rugs for lounging, embroidered pillows, and stunning, richly colored, expensive tapestries draped excessively all around the cavernous space. Ornate silver pitchers and cups sit on trays, beckoning one to sip thick, mysterious drinks. Candles housed in bronze with gorgeous perforated designs cast an enigmatic glow on the substantial yet temporary walls.

Abraham was resting in the door of his tent in the heat of the day, when he looked up and noticed three men nearby. He jumped up, bowed before them, and, after washing their feet, invited the men to stay for a bite to eat. This gesture of respect was so lovely, so honorable. As he rushed back to the tent he told Sarah, "Hurry! Bake some bread for our guests!" A servant prepared a calf, Abraham spread out a sumptuous feast, and he served his guests in the shade of the trees. There is nothing like Middle Eastern hospitality.

One of these men was "the angel of the Lord." Many scholars believe this is one of several theophanies in the Old Testament, also known as a pre-incarnate visit from Jesus. This makes my heart jump! Here Jesus was, personally paying Abraham and Sarah a visit, about to deliver good news, and enjoying an intimate meal. I like his style.

Here's what comes next in Genesis 18:9–10:

"Where is Sarah, your wife?" the visitors asked.

"She's inside the tent," Abraham replied.

Then one of them said, "I will return to you about this time next year, and your wife, Sarah, will have a son!"

How sublime is this incredible promise—this loving delivery of impossibly good news. Note that he said *Sarah* will have the son, not through Hagar; and it's not simply a spiritual son, but one of flesh and blood. He would share Sarah's DNA and come from Sarah's womb the old-fashioned way. He reiterated the literal promise made so long ago under a dusting of stars and revealed his plans to flesh it out his way—not the way Sarah tried to finagle it.

This was not new information to either Abraham or Sarah, but it likely resurrected conflicting feelings of hope rising and excitement building, alongside fear and disillusionment. Sarah was afraid to feel, to accept, to believe God's goodness to them.

Check out her response after hearing those words, this prophecy aimed like an arrow directly at Sarah's threadbare heart:

> Sarah was listening to this conversation from the tent. Abraham and Sarah were both very old by this time, and Sarah was long past the age of having children. So she laughed silently to herself and said, "How could a worn-out woman like me enjoy such pleasure, especially when my master—my husband—is also so old?" (Gen. 18:10–12)

Sarah laughed, although I'm guessing it was more of a snort. Or one of those *tch* sounds, *psshhh*, "I'm so sure," or any other appropriate accompaniment to a sneer—whatever exits our mouths when we hear something that sounds ridiculous, or sounds like someone trying to pass off a lie. Some saliva probably landed on the tent wall.

Sarah laughed, not joyfully but bitterly. How could she possibly be blessed with a child, considering her life's circumstances? They'd loomed large and cast a shadow on every corner of her life. She had a hardened and tired heart, which once held on to hope but had gradually let it go like the fine desert sand through her fingers. It was from this dry soil, this weary place, that her scoffing laughter sprang.

I know this bitterness well. I have endured the empty exhaustion of being denied my heart's desire. The despair and weariness that come from absorbing the punches life throws at you. You feel like you're in the corner of a boxing ring with blood running down your lopsided swollen eye. There are sweat and tears and no hope of victory against the heaving hulk in the opposite corner. There is no seeing straight, no thinking straight—only agony. You feel the hot breath, the shouting of encouragement, the screaming of those who want to help you get back up, to help you live, but it all gets drowned out by bleak circumstances, the endless jabs to the face, the gut, the heart. I know what it's like, when all you see is what or who is against you. There appears to be no way to fight back, no way to win, no way to catch a breath, much less overcome.

Maybe that's how Sarah felt as she hid inside the tent. Past menopause. Married to a one-hundred-year-old husband. Botched surrogacy. Homeless. It was not looking very probable, much less possible. It had been twenty-four years since she first heard the promise of a baby boy, the promise that she would birth the beginning of a great nation. Or was it a fairy tale? A figment of her imagination? Had the desert heat gotten to her that day? Had she downed one too many gorgeous goblets of Mediterranean wine? Did she hear correctly? Because God should have shown up by now. But instead he had let her womb dry up, and now it was too late to conceive a baby, too late to hang on to the fulfillment of an aging promise.

Sarah was up against an impossible wall, and so the spiteful chuckle tumbled forth. She just couldn't see past the immediate impossible circumstances and into the eternal unseen reality. At least not yet . . .

After this, in his kindness, God asked Abraham an unexpected question: "Why did Sarah laugh?" He called her out for harboring sour thoughts and small-mindedness toward God's abilities, toward his very word. Even though she had laughed silently and asked the question only to herself, God heard her loud and clear. He heard her silent bitterness, her unbelief, her mockery of his goodness. He heard her inwardly focused misery and witnessed the rolling of her eyes. And he hears mine.

This is something God does even now, as I allow him to perform heart surgery on me. He has totally convicted me about my decision to focus on the terrible rather than the wonderful. I have too often chosen a lack of faith, chosen to squeeze my eyes shut and wallow in the reeking funk of self-pity. I have too often made the decision to let sharp, resentful words reside in my inner dialogue.

Snarky thoughts and cranky commentary have been sneaking around in my head and heart for some time. I have brushed them off as humor. I have given myself a break because, after all, my kid died, you know. I have compared myself with others who are grieving for various reasons and have graded myself on the curve, believing that if anyone deserves a self-indulgent attitude, it's me.

I have welcomed those ugly little phrases to hover around the recesses of my brain. I've kept feelings of rancor in a bowl by the door, ready to be passed out like Halloween candy. I've nurtured them. I have given them space, made their beds, and fluffed their pillows. Probably the worst thing about it is that I have felt justified through it all. God, forgive me.

You know when we say, "God knows my heart"? Well, he actually does, and it should freak us out. I'm pretty positive that's usually not what we want it to mean. We most often say it to defend our sloppy, selfish actions, using it as a flimsy excuse one can't argue with. We can do or say the most ridiculous of things and feel completely justified . . . "It's cool, God knows my heart."

The prophet Jeremiah said the heart is desperately wicked. Oh Lord, don't I know it. I may be a pastor's wife, but my heart is as wicked as the next girl's. I am filled up with selfishness, contempt, impatience, pride, entitlement, and, honestly, the list goes on.

When God asked why Sarah laughed, he had already seen her heart, and it was not pretty. He wasn't about to let her off the hook, not because he wanted to point out a flaw or because he'd taken offense. He wasn't angling to feel smart or look good in front of the others. No, God cared about how Sarah received the promise he gave to her. That's why he exposed her reaction. He wanted more for her than bitter resignation, so he confronted her with her hidden sin. Desiring to swap out what was corroding Sarah's soul for what can bring life and wholeness, he asked, "Why did Sarah laugh? Abe, I heard your wife snorting in the next tent over. What gives?" (See Gen. 18:13–14.)

In these sticky, messy hearts of ours, there's never just one little sin; there's a whole string of them. Like when you think you've found the mouse in your kitchen that's been snacking on the granola, and the thought crosses your mind that by itself it's actually kind of cute and maybe you should let it live. Adorable little fella with the pink ears and tail, he's not so bad. But soon you discover that there's a whole nasty nest full of them, and they've been pooping and reproducing in your lingerie drawer.

Sarah had another "mouse" following on the tail of her first snafu of chagrined laughter—a big fat fib. When confronted, Sarah lied, straight to God's face! She was afraid, we read, so she denied it all.

"Wasn't me. Don't know what you're talking about!" (See Genesis 18:15.)

I'm so thankful my worst moments aren't canonized in Scripture for all to read! But honestly, thank you, Sarah, for letting us learn from you. Thank you for your candor.

Sarah laughed—yikes. God asked her why she did so— yikes. But now, in my opinion, this is the pièce de résistance. This part of the story is so funny, but at the same time totally fear inducing. After the fib Sarah throws down, the Lord said to her, "No, you did laugh."

Wouldn't you be mortified? I can see his face, display- ing a parental look that says, "Don't even try to pull a fast one. I've got your number, sweetie pie." He didn't let it go but made a point, and the point was a beautiful thing: God heard her bitter laughter, and he wanted her to know that nothing was too marvelous for him. He had exciting news for her and wanted to present it to his beloved daughter. She could have taken it in her hands with joy and wonder, opened the gift with glee. But instead she received it with folded arms, with pursed lips, with rejection.

Oh Sarah, I get it. Me too. How foreign good news sounds when the heart is pulsing sorrow with every beat, when all around is opposition, when life completely stinks. How many of us are there right now? We are tired; our faith is stretched thin; we thought we knew what our place was on this earth. We thought we knew what we believed.

Maybe we've failed to obey God in certain areas, or we've been let down by someone we were counting on. Or maybe the one thing we wanted and were convinced God would give us still dangles in the distance—unreachable, taunting, tormenting. We feel like Sarah, old and tired and sad and beaten down. We secretly laugh in mockery when we think of blessings coming our way. We laugh in disbelief. We have begun the unraveling of faith, working the pile of loose thread into a picture of despair.

But God hears us laughing. He hears the sound of our bitter scoffing and wants to call us out on it, wants us to come out of our inward-focused pity party.

I'm so convicted by this. My tendency is toward self-preservation, but true to the counterintuitive way God often works, it has been a tremendous encouragement and blessing to lift my head and listen hard through the tent wall, to receive the rebuke, to be reminded that nothing is too marvelous for my Lord.

You know how, in the book of John, Jesus said that unless a grain of wheat falls to the ground and dies, it can't live? That's what I'm talking about. Doing what you think will save yourself actually works against you. Think about your body. When our tendency is toward self-preservation, we figure lying curled up in bed after a birth or a hard workout is the best thing we can do for our bodies—to protect them from further injury or strain. It feels good in the moment. But in the long run, it works against us. Muscles atrophy and we become sick and weak because various parts of our bodies begin to shut down from lack of use.

Or it's like a marriage in which one or both spouses are merely concerned with protecting themselves, as if marriage were a contract, not a covenant. They think getting their own way, whether by physically, emotionally, or even financially withholding themselves from the other, will result in personal happiness and satisfaction. The marriage inevitably crumbles when it's fueled by self-protection, but that same sickly relationship becomes strong and begins to shine when one spouse is brave enough to step out of the way of self-preservation and choose the way of death to self—whether in the form of respect, service, or forgiveness. It doesn't make sense, but it's true. It's another way we exercise our faith, because it takes faith to come out of the self-defensiveness of grief and disappointment.

There are still bitter parts in me he wants to mine out. He wants to completely free me from self-pity, free me from immobilizing melancholy, free me from brooding about terrible memories that push me deeper into the stink. I can feel them being chipped away, sometimes with the finesse of a tool meant for uncovering precious gems. Minute movements expose bits of precious beauty:

realizations of biblical truth and gentle reminders of Jesus' love for me and my place as his adopted daughter. Other parts are being excavated with a big old grubby pickax, hard chunks flying, inducing sweat, tears, and piles of waste that were getting in the way of the good stuff. Inside there is a vein of gold, the gleaming slash that brightens the surrounding dullness of the hard-packed earth. It's never a neat or clean affair when your self-righteous pity party is brought into the light.

"Life is hard, then you die."

Why did you laugh?

"Apparently God doesn't hear my prayers, so I'll be sitting this one out."

Why did you laugh?

"Sure would be fun to have more kids. Too bad mine keep dying."

Why did you laugh?

"The dance recital sounds fun. But it's for people whose kids are alive, and, well, mine's dead, so . . ."

Why did you laugh?

I make snide comments in my mind, flimsy attempts at humor that only serve to showcase my emotional desperation. I sometimes behave as if I'm the only one on earth who has had her heart ripped out, but I've been busted. I'm stepping into Sarah's place right now, busted for eavesdropping with disregard for keeping my eyes on that which is unseen, busted for staying in a place of stony heart and inflexible vision, busted for laughing at God's promised goodness with mockery.

God wants not only to free me from what comes between us but also to give me a hope that draws me nearer to himself. Nearness to God results in a banquet of peace beyond understanding, with a heaping side of joy. He wants to give me laughter—hilarious, sidesplitting, tears-running-down-my-face, can't-get-a-breath, bladder-busting laughter. The kind you can only find amid the plans of the Maker, amid the anticipation of present and coming glory.

Thank you, Jesus, for not letting us continue in our flesh when we feel so entitled to it. We feel like we are only human and "just trying to survive here, people"; but he disciplines those he loves. Instead of being vindicated by a heavenly visitor because life had been so sad in so many ways, Sarah got set straight.

God didn't give her a break and say, "Yeah, I'd laugh too. It's cool. You're old, and life is hard." No, he said, "Why did you laugh? I've got this. And don't lie. I heard you." He saw something Sarah wasn't humanly able to, and he sees something that's beyond my vision as well.

He was planning to turn Sarah's mourning to joy. He's planning to turn my mourning and your mourning to joy, the kind of joy we can't drum up on our own. The kind of joy that requires faith in his goodness for an awesome future. Because when I woke up on a Monday morning and put my bathing suit on underneath my clothes for a surf date with my husband but landed instead at the hospital, it took faith to survive the impossible, nightmarish days that followed.

When I'm choking on memories of my lifeless darling girl, of her limp body in my arms, of how I handed her over to the men in suits waiting to carry her out my front door in the predawn hours, when every sunrise for the rest of my life will remind me of that night of radical loss, it takes faith to see past the inky blackness. When my skin aches to feel Daisy's face on mine again, when I remember what it felt like to kiss her lifeless forehead, growing colder by the minute, it takes faith to process the longing. When I see my daughter's best friends playing together and growing up without her, when I know by experience that life changes in the blink of an eye, when I'm left bleeding out from watching cancer slay my daughter bit by bit, when I set the table for three, not four, it takes faith to see beyond the present sadness.

It takes faith to get out of bed in the morning, faith to let my guard down. It takes faith to love someone new, faith to face another day with a destroyed and suspicious heart. It takes faith to move forward in life, and, truly, it takes faith to not laugh in bitterness, dwelling on hostile circumstances.

Here is why Sarah's shenanigans in the tent encourage me, reminding me of something that allows the smile to creep slowly across my face. The only way to get that essential faith, to experience the healing truth, is to go straight to the mouth of God. Straight to the Lord who came up Sarah's driveway and had a cheeseburger at her tent, straight to the Maker of the universe, the Master Designer.

It's true—faith comes by hearing the Word of God. It's necessary to continually make the choice to open my ears. Sarah eavesdropped through the tent, straining to hear what God had to say to her family, but I have the whole Scripture bound in leather. I have about twenty-five copies in my home, in any translation, size, or color I fancy that day. Oh, how thick-skulled can we be, when the tools we need to survive and thrive have been lavished on us but we choose to ignore them. Oh, the crazy fun, the electric anticipation of when we set our eyes on Jesus, when we swap burdens for freedom, when we give attention to the Word of God speaking love over us.

Through the Word we have the honor of seeing the other side of Sarah's encounter in the tent that day, what happened at the end of the story. Though Sarah couldn't, we can already feel baby Isaac's downy head snuggled in Sarah's wrinkled neck. We hear the stirring and hilarious laughter that follows the bitter. But we get to laugh too. We have heaven promised; we have redemption and joy and comfort coming our way! We have peace and freedom and the realization of every deep desire, the unfolding of the future of the world all laid out for us.

Can we, just for a second, imagine this as it pertains to us—twenty-first-century women with modern heartaches and modern problems? Can we, just as Sarah's womb and arms were filled with goodness, believe our own hearts will be also? Shall we just linger in this thought, in this picture of what's possible when we aren't homing in on the difficult, on the bitter? Can we peek in the back of the Book; can we go back over all the sure words of prophecy; can we read of the life of our Savior and scoop it all into our chests like a mound of warm sand on the beach and scream, "Yes! I'll take it! It's mine! It's mine because of the goodness of the Lord, the grace he poured out, because he is love!"

And, nestling in that pile of warmth, we can in sweet surrender lay down our heads, feel the sun radiating comfort on our tired backs, hear the echo of our newly resuscitated heartbeat, and bask in the tenderness of a Father who loves us enough to get in our business.

Six

YES, PLEASE

As a mom, one of the most beautiful things I can hear from the mouth of any of my babies is "yes." I spend months, even years, giving direction and punctuating it with: "Say, 'Okay, Mama,' 'Yes, Mama.'" It tells me they heard me, whether or not they fully understand. It says they agree with the goodness I want to lavish on them. It's the acceptance of what I have planned, the cooperation and partnership for a peaceful and happy home. I want my kids to acknowledge me, to agree with me, so that I can bless them and keep them safe.

My son, Isaiah, used to have a lisp. The most darling lisp there ever was. Whenever I would ask him to do something for me, or tell him some important information that needed to be acknowledged, or correct a bit of naughtiness, I would kneel down to his level, look in his sparkly aquamarine eyes shining behind fringes of white fluffy hair, and wait to hear it.

"Yeth, Mama."

Melt my heart. He heard me. He agreed with me. He could now move forward into blessing and peace with us, who loved him. We made our every decision for his good. We fed and cared for and disciplined and guided and blessed and provided for and doted on and sacrificed for him.

Sometimes it's hard to get those babies to say yes. Or even yeth. For whatever reason, sometimes they don't think what I have to offer is the best. They decide they know better. They don't think they need rest or nutrition or to be taught self-control. They can't see beyond their immediate desires. They don't understand that if they obey Mama and get in the high chair, they will receive a treat. They don't believe that if they stop wiggling long enough for me to strap them in the car seat, we can go to the beach.

Just yesterday I was getting my daughter Fifi into the car. We were heading to the beach to meet friends, the same beach where my fourteen-year-old son works as a junior counselor at a surf camp. It was going to be perfect—there would be gorgeous weather, unusually warm water, and a darling brother to give her kisses and piggyback rides. My plans for her were good.

Fifi, however, was standing in her seat, knees locked so that her baby fat spread around north and south. There was no telling the difference between thigh and calf.

"Time to sit down in your seat, so we can see Bro-bro at the beach."

"Hi," she said in her tiny fairy voice.

She was so cute I could hardly stand it. "Please sit down, so we can go."

"Hi."

"Sit down."

"Hi."

Okay, not so cute anymore. "We can't go to the beach until you sit in your seat."

"Hi."

I watched her repeatedly refuse to agree with my plan, but even though she was high on the naughty chart, I could still have eaten her face with a spoon. Gosh, I love her so much. But this is not the seventies anymore; we have car seats now. Until she agreed with me there would be no sand castles, no brother kisses, no sandy peanut butter sandwiches.

Toddlers have little comprehension for the consequences of disobedience. They haven't experienced the disappointment of discovering a skateboard with rusty trucks from being left out in the rain, or the de-lamination of the bottom of a boogie board left in the sun for days. They also don't yet understand the blessing of obedience. Fifi didn't realize that a trip to the beach requires an agreement, a "Yes, Mama, buckle me in."

"Believe me!" I wanted to shout. "I love you more than I ever thought possible! I threw up for you, got stretch marks for you, haven't slept in years for you! I make every decision in this household to benefit you, to go along with my master plan of raising you up fully loved and fully equipped to succeed in life and love and wisdom. Just agree. Please!"

It takes agreement to deepen relationship; agreement lets us move on to bigger and better things. And if you think about it, even though I was looking for Fifi to say yes, to choose the love-deepening, relationship-building result of walking in agreement, in the end, she wasn't doing the heavy lifting. It was me. It was my communication with her, my bending to her level, my heart beating in anticipation as I hoped for a sign that she was tracking with me. I was the one doing all these things. I was the one with plans for her; I was the one steering her life.

Aren't we just that way with God? In the end, it's not so much about what *we* do, but about agreeing with what *he* is doing and wants to do for us. In that nod, in that "Yes, Papa," we are brought closer in our abiding with him. It cultivates the pure and childlike trust in the One who holds our future, who offers joy and life and laughter, who carries us forward. He is offering freedom from fear and the bondage of sadness. He is kneeling down, saying, "I know the way. I *am* the way. Just say yes."

My favorite yes of all time was spoken by a poor teenage country girl. This radically real young woman blows my mind. She was definitely the closest thing to P31 you can get. She was virtuous; she was strong. She was kind; she was faithful. She was steadfast and righteous and probably could sing and paint and dance, but mostly this girl was brave—laugh-in-the-face-of-danger brave. Like Corrie ten Boom, Joan of Arc, and Amy Carmichael, but cooler. She was the one willing to risk it all for Jesus— figuratively and literally.

Mary. You know the one, the mother of Jesus. I can't wait to meet her in heaven. (I've asked God if Daisy could be introduced sometime soon. I ask that often, if Daisy is getting to hang out with fabulous people in heaven.)

Shall we set the scene again? I picture Mary absent-mindedly sweeping a packed dirt floor with a sparse straw broom, in reverie about living in the future home of her betrothed. Dutifully performing the last of the chores before she settles on her pallet, one last candle lit, the evening still from the day's usual steady hum of family life. Rustic kitchen tools hang on earthen walls lovingly plastered by common, hardworking hands. Her family's tiny apartment adjoins with countless others, perched on a hillside. Little windows like a smattering of tiny eyes blinked out from a rambling communal dwelling place on the outskirts of a sleepy village. I imagine Mary's cheeks flushed with youth, her strong, young body covered in simple homespun, likely a thin line of careful embroidery stitches lining the hem—a hint of beauty amid the plain. Perhaps she holds something precious on a string around her neck, hidden from curious siblings' eyes—a ring from a beloved grandmother, maybe? Or a roughly made key to the hope chest she will bring to her wedded home very soon. There is optimism, expectancy, and promise in her purity, in her loveliness. An unmistakable, quiet strength. And then the gasp that pierces the silence as she is made aware of her cosmic visitor.

Mary was quite young when the angel came to her. Some say as young as thirteen to fifteen years old. According to Luke chapter 1, Gabriel the messenger angel appeared to her, greeted her joyfully, and pronounced her a favored woman. Apparently angels aren't very subtle, nor are they ones for beating around the bush. Young Mary was confused and disturbed, which is not too surprising, seeing as this mysterious messenger was a huge, shiny nonhuman who hadn't been there just a second ago. Talk about caught off guard!

Gabriel pressed in with more enigmatic news, reminding her of two very important yet perplexing things. "Don't be afraid," he said. "You have found favor with God." Then he slipped in the most electrifying, rapturous, exalted thing a Jewish woman could ever have hoped to hear: She would be mother of the Messiah. And, oh, by the way, he would be called Son of the Most High, he would reign over Israel forever, and his kingdom would never end. Boom!

What?! Wait, hold on, back up. *Don't be afraid?* Listen, Gabe, being pregnant is scary. You get nine months of sick and tired and grumpy and itchy and chubby and swollen and lost continence. Plus, you look like an Oompa Loompa and waddle like a penguin. And don't get me started on birth! The pain, the mess, the animal sounds that come from your gut . . . Sheesh! Don't be afraid, my eye.

But Miracle Mary didn't have merely a first pregnancy

and birth to be afraid of. She had a truckload of obstacles ahead. She faced ostracism in her community as her pregnancy would appear to be unfaithfulness to her betrothed. She faced potential stoning by her father and getting ditched by her fiancé. She conceivably could have been left in the cold, hungry and uncared for, alone save for her promised baby boy. Mary knew there would be a hard road ahead. The whispers and stares of the neighbors, the loss of reputation, the trepidation of raising the very Son of God. She had every reason to fear. Every reason to say, "Nah, thanks anyway, but that's totally out of my comfort zone." Every reason to weigh the pros and cons and go with her own plan—her safe, clean, conventional, and financially beneficial plan.

Yet she didn't. She looked into the eyes of that terrifying and glorious celestial being and asked one question: "But how can this happen? I am a virgin." Oh, Mary, can I be you for a day? Can I just throw aside all self-preservation tendencies, all inhibition, all vanity and earthly reason, and just be you? She didn't ask what was in it for her; she didn't ask who would take care of her. She didn't ask how she could hide the truth. She merely wanted to know how it would be made possible.

And her question was answered. Gabriel explained the power of the Holy Spirit, boosted his credibility with more miraculous news about Mary's elderly cousin Elizabeth becoming pregnant, then said something we now see on mugs and T-shirts and bumper stickers. Something that rolls off our tongues when we want to present a tidy Christian response, when we want to appear righteous and sanguine. He said the thing we believe for others but seldom for ourselves, something of enormous magnitude that is often overlooked because of our tendency to hear the Word, yet not know the Speaker.

Gabriel leaned his great gleaming head down toward this plucky teenager and looked her in the eye, holding her gaze in the stillness of the Galilean night. Then, with all conviction and adoration and fierce loyalty, he said, "For nothing is impossible with God."

Next comes one of my favorite moments in the history of women. Mary, in an act of worship, of truth, of devotion, of abandon, and of terrifying trust, said, "I am the Lord's servant. May everything you have said about me come true" (Luke 1:38).

Yes. She said yes.

When's the last time we said that to Jesus? When's the last time we looked him square in the face and said, "I am your servant. Take me with you. Lead me into the lion's den, the king's court, the ark, the promised land. Carry me while I care for orphans, defy enemies, risk my life for truth. Accept my meager offering, a drink of cold water, the washing of your feet with my hair and tears, the fragrance of embalming spices pungent in the darkest hour. Take me straight to the cross with you, for I know you are good."

Yes is a powerful word, and it is packed with meaning. Mary's yes professed she was honored to carry the Messiah in her womb, willing to face shame and the unknown. Mary's yes meant she would be uncomfortably traveling through the countryside at full term for several days due to a government census. Mary's yes said she would birth her firstborn son in a makeshift barn with only an unwashed trough to lay him in. Her yes was an unwitting invitation to strange shepherds visiting her sacred birthing room, filling it with the stench of sweat and dung and wool.

Mary's yes also brought blessing along with the mysterious conception of her new life. It gave Mary so much more than she could have imagined, holy little gifts cloaked in the ordinary. Mary, who memorized the face of Love Come Down, surrounded by the gentle contentment of livestock shifting their weight and nibbling hay. Mary, honored to tenderly change holy diapers, to wash hummus from Jesus' full, young face, to teach him to count. Mary, who breathed in the scent of his brunette curls and sang lullabies ever more softly so that he would lean into her warmth a bit closer. Mary, fortunate to hold Jesus' small, soft brown hand, to teach him the names of the animals they saw while walking to Torah school. Mary, who watched her boy grow in wisdom as he spent time at the synagogue, then witnessed his face transforming from boy to man. Mary, privileged to witness the

Gift of Heaven right under her own roof, right under her own skin.

Mary—who witnessed miracles, who followed faithfully, who stayed by Jesus' side even unto his death . . . she would have missed all this loveliness had she succumbed to comfort, to disobedience.

In her yes, not knowing the outcome of her life or her son's, she remained faithful as she watched her grown son work humbly as a carpenter, choosing not to take a wife. She pondered truth and believed God's Word. Her yes didn't mean she understood it all, but it meant she understood God's sovereignty.

Mary. Her life was such a mix of highs and lows, of the mundane and the miraculous. Such a life of faith and blessing, yet one so full of hardship. I want to be like Mary. I want to say with conviction in the face of the supernatural and the earthly, with anticipation of greatness and blessed obedience, with a love song bursting forth from my deepest heart, "I am yours. Be it done to me as you say."

As each day without Daisy goes by, a choice lies before me. Shall I agree with God and move forward? Or shall I live in denial, stubbornly unable to receive blessings or be a blessing?

In the first year after her death, I had multiple dreams

about her. In each dream she would be at a different point in time of her life, or really, of her sickness. I could always tell what stage she was in, whether it was before diagnosis or during remission or treatment, by her hair length. Sometimes I would dream we were playing with stuffed animals in a tepee or laughing on a bed. Other times we would be in a hospital together, discussing cartoons and card games. She would be subdued in some dreams, as if she was still sick, and in others she was her usual spunky self, making faces and full of energy.

One morning I woke up after dreaming extensively about her. This dream I will never forget. I could smell her, feel her, hear her. We were together, best friends, hearts connected. Then I dreamed about her sickness, the countless therapies, and the way she died. The dream lasted so long that I got confused. When I awoke and realized I had been dreaming, I felt so relieved. I was relieved that it was all just a horrible nightmare, the whole cancer and dying thing. I lay there thinking how real and detailed the dreadful dream had been and felt so thankful my Daisy Love was actually in the next room asleep in her bed. In the early morning blur of dawn, as my scattered thoughts worked to organize themselves into comprehension, it took me a good five minutes to realize I was wrong—that, yes, it had been a dream, but it was also real. The devastation, the disappointment, came flooding back in a torrent of horror and tears and denial.

What was there for me to do? What does a woman say to the One who hung the moon? When Job had nothing left but a pile of ashes and a piece of pottery to scratch his sores, when he had questioned and argued and lamented and was left a broken man with nothing before a God who is everything, what did he do? He worshipped. And so, in the fuzzy gloom of the predawn hour, I gave what sliver of myself I had left to God. I said yes.

Yes, I trust you.

Yes, I believe you when you say there is something so much better coming that all will pale in comparison.

Yes, you will be with me in the valley of the shadow of death.

Yes, you will walk me through the frightening austerity of life.

Yes, you love me.

Yes, you made the ultimate sacrifice for me.

Yes, you are real, you are good, you are the Beginning and End.

Yes, you have not left me alone. You see me, you've collected my tears in your bottle, and you have future plans for me.

Like Mary, I look forward to what the yes brings. I choose not to miss the blessing of obedience. I want to witness the miraculous; I want to find the comfort in the mundane. From Fifi's tiny giggle to Isaiah's boy-man hug, from the scent of my husband to the perfect fit of a baby's body curled up in mine. The cradle of warmth under a billowing blanket, and the sharing of it with someone precious. The strength of a marriage that has been tried by fire, the depth of wisdom suffering brings, the healing hope that speaks of the goodness of God and life and love beyond circumstances.

The yes doesn't always make sense. We don't fully understand how God works, but we read in 2 Corinthians 1:20: "For all of God's promises have been fulfilled in Christ with a resounding 'Yes!' And through Christ, our 'Amen' (which means 'Yes') ascends to God for his glory."

Yes. He's the One who made us; he's the One who sacrificed for us. He's the One who is working redemption and goodness and healing and boundless love, not us. And our agreeing glorifies him? I can never make sense of the way things add up in Jesus. It's all him, all his goodness, his worthiness, and yet when we agree, we get a piece of the glory pie. Unbelievable.

Yes, Abba. Yes.

Seven

LIONHEARTED

"Why are you afraid? You have so little faith!"

—MATTHEW 8:26

My biblical heroines, my fellow sufferers, are rock-solid. We've seen them go from weakness to strength, shame to dignity. From heartsickness to happiness, we link arms and walk together in the tight-knit clique of girl power. Together we are bold; we are defiantly joyful. We are kicking butt and taking names—until the "Eye of the Tiger" music comes to a screeching halt, and we are faced unexpectedly with fear. Fears lie dormant. They have been there all along but awaken like Bilbo's dragon. Just when we think we are getting somewhere in our journey, fears stand in the way of great treasure. We can't go any further in our discussion of strength, dignity, and laughter without confronting fear.

Fear. An ugly, nauseous word. Fear blows into our worlds uninvited and surrounds, thick like dog breath. It presses down, lies heavily on our chests, strangling and choking. It desires to paralyze, to make us sick. No longer can we walk poised. Fear trips our confident strides, and they become unwieldy. Hemmed in by an almost visible, stinking cloud of fear, we find ourselves self-focused, scratching to look out for number one. We believe the lies of self-preservation; we become tricked into distrusting Jesus.

Fear takes no prisoners. Fear just goes for the jugular, striking where it hurts. Fear leaves no one untouched, zeroing in on the most vulnerable parts of us, the most fragile. And the most costly.

I have a dear friend whose husband once got in a nasty motorcycle accident, and now, every single time any member of her family is on the road, she is stifled by fear and unable to think of anything else. Another friend faces the dread of miscarrying yet again, having her deepest desire stolen repeatedly. She fears the sight of blood, which threatens to rip her heart out. Others of my friends have battled loneliness, health problems, career loss, depression, cancer, sudden deaths in the family, and husbands with addictions. Satan always goes for the chink in the armor, threatening us with loathsome thoughts, with wild imaginations, with taunting and the cruel dangling of life's horrors in front of our faces.

I knew fear intimately as a little girl. I endured many years petrified of the dark, thanks to scary movies and an overactive imagination. I would lie awake, sure I had seen something slithering in the shadows. I would nearly suffocate myself under the covers, believing that if I could hide long enough, they would protect me from whatever was lying in wait to harm me. It was more than just a childhood phase. After I got married I still turned on every light in the house on the nights when Britt went out of town, which were often. I'd play worship music on the stereo to calm my anxieties, but since those were the days before digital music, I also had to get up every fifty-four minutes or so to push play again. One night I was so tormented by fear, I threw one-year-old Isaiah in the car at midnight and drove across town to my mom's house to sleep in her room with her.

My list of fears doesn't stop at sleeping alone in the house. I've been afraid of becoming a victim of road rage, afraid of bad guys coming into my house. I've let panic overcome me when my children were out of my sight for longer than a few minutes, or when my husband was driving home late at night. I've been paralyzed with trepidation over large dogs, bears on hiking trails, and shark sightings near my local surf spot.

Some of these fears are legit but unwarranted—I've never been bitten by a dog, shark, or bear, and I've never had my house broken into. Others are silly but unfortunately justifiable, such as my fear of getting bucked off a horse or being walked in on while peeing in a public restroom, since these things have happened to me more than once. But perhaps the most outlandish fear I've had is that a psycho, demon-possessed person might pull a gun on my husband while he's preaching in the pulpit. It's something I've worried about ever since a bloody, drunk guy covered in stab wounds charged him onstage at our college group one night. Yes, that actually happened.

So many unknowns, such a veritable buffet of things

to fear. But, having lived a life of relative peace and safety, none of these things were ever actually worth the time and energy required to worry, to freak out, to agitate, to grind my teeth over—until the day it all changed, when this mother's greatest fear was realized.

Fear has been a committed, malicious attendant since Daisy's first diagnosis. It's such a wretched, unwelcome thing. An oily fiend. Yet I have become well acquainted with it, with that unmistakable metallic tang of horror, rudely assaulting every cell of my body. As fear has fermented and matured, it has evolved and taken on different feelings, different reactions. It has become a familiar sour taste in my mouth, a scent that causes my stomach to lurch.

Cancer is an infamously moving target, carrying with it myriad atrocious possible side effects and outcomes— all unknown, yet all disfiguring. The side effects and survival rates became overflowing vessels of pain and sorrow, balancing what was most valuable to me on earth in their menacing claws. It was shockingly unfair.

For three and a half years, every time I saw the doctor's number come up on my phone, I felt sick. Every time the scent of the antimicrobial soap in the hospital wafted past, my heart raced. Every lab report, every drop of chemo being pushed into Daisy's veins, every sharply stinging shot that made her cry brought a rush of choking sensations. Even the vials for her precious blood samples induced alarm.

But the pinnacle of the unspeakable thing we call cancer treatment was the scans. Like clockwork, starting about a week before a scheduled CT scan, I would lose my mind. I felt catatonic for days, steeling every nerve to receive what could potentially be devastating news and would indicate whether Daisy's cancer had grown or shrunk. It was like opening the closet door after having seen evidence of the most hideous monster you can imagine. Was it home? Would it come out this time and rip your head off, tear your heart out? Or would it have gone out for a quick lunch, lulling you into a false sense of security, only to arrive back at any moment? In the days before a scan, I didn't eat and could hardly take care of myself, let alone my family. I couldn't think about anything other than the looming verdict. I shut down, heavily.

The crazy thing is, now my worst fear has been realized. My daughter's life was overcome by cancer, snuffed out with a ragged final breath inches from my face. I have buried my most precious little girl. And, depending on the angle from which I look, depending on the lens through which I choose to peer, I could conceivably say it was worth being afraid. I could argue that I should, in fact, stay afraid as a form of protection, because life is brutal and good things don't last.

Or I could say that God was with me, that he received Daisy into his arms, that he carried us through the valley of the shadow of death and will continue to be present in our time of need. It's my choice how I want to view it. Either way, fear is real, and though the vast majority of our fears will never be realized, sometimes wretched stuff happens.

Fears abound in most of us, yet we keep them hidden. We nourish and feed them like parasites. We hold on to them, believing keeping them close will help our situation, as if fretting hard enough will make it all better. We are convinced worrying can heal or save or keep our loved ones from harm. We spend hours mulling over potential circumstances and wringing our hands. We sleep with the covers over our heads and every light on. We are haunted. We are left exhausted, raw, and no better off for all the freaking out.

I have to be honest: I still become fearful sometimes. I now know deep sorrow. I have tasted death and confusion and bitter grief. I know that what I once thought only happened to other people can happen to me. I used to see the lady with the cancer kid and think, *Oh, how terrible*, but the next thing I knew, I was the one pushing an IV pole down the hospital corridor with my own bald daughter and her teddy bear. Life changes in a blink.

So much of what we think is solid here on earth is not. Anything can happen. I am not out of the woods, and neither are you. Hurt and death and sorrow and disaster happen every day, and they could come knocking on my door again. There is no guarantee that my other two children will make it to adulthood, or that the baby I'm carrying in my womb as I write this will be born alive. There's no guarantee that I won't get cancer or have my leg bitten off by a shark or crash my car into a ditch. Sometimes, much too often, the fear I wear, like an ill-fitting, bulky garment while trying to swim, overwhelms me and drags me down.

Anything can be the catalyst. I feel the familiar churning pit in my stomach, and soon I feel the urge to use the bathroom because I'm anxious, worried, queasy. Do you know what I mean? Just yesterday Fifi fell down, hurting her belly on the left side. Nausea settled in as I remembered how a fall had burst Daisy's tumor, on the same side as Fifi's new bruise. Cue the curtains. I can actually see the lights fading now that deep grief and loss are my constant companions.

It doesn't take much, usually, for me to go dark. I joke with my husband and close friends about my PTSD. Hyperventilating over a bug bite on my baby? Oh, that's just my PTSD acting up. In a catatonic state because I was sure my son got kidnapped? Yeah, PTSD. But it's no joke. I go so quickly into the freak-out zone. The smallest thing threatens to drown me in fear, take over my thoughts. It keeps me immobile, eyes wild.

In fact, when Fifi was three months old, she contracted whooping cough. There was an epidemic in my area, and my homeschooled son had brought it home from junior high youth group. Babies under six months old are at risk of death from this freight train of an illness, and there had already been a death in our city caused by it.

❧ I watched helplessly as my tiny girl struggled to catch her breath after each coughing spell. That's where the whooping part comes in. Her body would expel every speck of air, and then, as she tried to breathe in, she would make a desperate whooping sound through constricted air passages. Every single hour she coughed laboriously, the spasms refusing to stop. Her face and lips would turn blue, her eyes frenetic, as she hysterically waved her arms around, looking to us to save her. Hourly we helped her catch her breath, blowing in her face at just the right time, triggering an infant's instinct to suck in air.

Needless to say, my heart dropped out of my chest every single time she turned blue. I felt the crazies rising up in me, body shaking at the thought of wrapping another baby in linen and laying her to rest. Hourly I raged against massive panic. I fought hard against the physical sensations, the frenzied attempts to help her. The intense blue-faced coughing went on for six weeks, then another five months of coughing fits without the whoop. I was mowed down by fear, totally and completely spent.

We survived whooping cough, but still, I find myself every now and then surrendering to this unknowable emotion of fear—handing my heart and soul and wellness to this sickening enemy. I might as well wrap them up and tie on a bow. I hand it all over, on a platter. "Here, Fear. Have it. Have all my well-being. Have my peace. Have my faith in God, while we're at it, because who needs faith when they have worry?" And I hate it. I hate myself for it. I hate the state it puts me in. I hate who I become after I give in to it.

Fear causes us to miss out on the beauty and joy that exists in every life. Fear robs, steals, pillages our very hearts and leaves behind a greasy film not removable by human hands. Fear is the unwelcome greedy guest, the depressing third wheel, the clinging darkness clouding the light of the Son. Fear takes all the joy out of today, sucks the life out of me and everyone around me—but worst of all, fear says, "I don't trust you; you are not good," to God.

I know I'm not the only one who has a list of fears. You might not have walked through cancer and bereavement, but maybe you're the woman who has blown it so hard that you're bracing yourself for the consequences of your sinful actions. What if you have experienced a violent breakup and now fear a hostile man? Or you've had addictions to substances or unhealthy behaviors or habitual lies and are too afraid to quit, fear begging you to carry on? What if you are so broken up inside over your wretchedness, over the sin you have hidden, over the pain you have caused, that you feel you can't go on, afraid that you have been rejected by God and anyone else who knows who you really are? Fear has got you in its vulgar grip.

What about the girl who feels unseen, unloved, over-looked, and fears being left alone? Or the one who appears so amazing on the outside and is applauded for her perfection but is a hot mess on the inside? The pretender who fears being found out?

Or maybe your life is awesome and wonderful, and you're afraid that it will come crashing down at any moment, for no apparent reason.

We all have fears. But that's not the end for us. Because you know what I know? You know what I overheard through the tent? Don't be afraid. Over and over in the Word, God said to his people, "Do not be afraid." Jesus repeatedly told his disciples, "Fear not."

This may sound like a pipe dream of boldness and courage, yet wearing fear like an everyday garment is no way to live. Though fear is a formidable and relentless monster, we can learn how to fight. We can learn to be guided by Jesus when we are held down, crushed, and suffocated.

I have learned to put down my Coke bottles and pick up my Truth lenses. Strength comes swiftly as I seek to know what is true about the whole business. Jesus said in John 14:27, "I am leaving you with a gift—peace of mind and heart. And the peace I give is a gift the world cannot give. So don't be troubled or afraid."

You who fear, do this with me. Lean closely enough to hear him and understand with clarity what he is saying to us. Let us make a trade; instead of storing up fears in our hearts, give them to Jesus. Pour them out at his feet, pooled and congealed. A disgusting virus to be rid of. Setting aside the fear of the future sets us free—and in it we realize we never had control in the first place.

By faith we receive in return for our fears a glorious truth: that he is for us, that he longs to give us peace, that he is right here with us offering to carry our burdens. By faith we hold these things; by faith we look at Jesus' track record and realize he can be trusted. By faith we see ourselves in light of the history of the world and realize there's a greater plan. By faith we obey his Word, knowing he is worthy, he is bigger than us, and he is love.

What a gift it is to know and believe he truly is our Shepherd, that he searches to find us when we're lost, fights wolves for us. I don't want to be defined by my circumstances or let them dictate my days. Do you? We can experience deep heartache and still experience exultant joy. We can daringly walk in who God made us to be and not be swallowed up by fear. And we don't walk alone. Our community of suffering provides comfort, yes, but it also ignites courage.

I want to take our friendship with Mary a little deeper. Let's look at some crucial and scary parts of her life a little more closely. Because Mary was dauntless in her yes. And Mary was favored in ways so inconsistent with how we understand blessings.

Not Mary the sinless, blond-haired, baby-blue-dress-wearing picture of placid perfection—Mary of serene loveliness, smiling with lips softly closed and head tilted just right. No, not her. The Mary I read of in Scripture is the one with guts, true grit, and unwavering faith in her Creator, the Master Storyteller.

Bold Mary—chosen not only for the most mysterious and honorable task a human can perform, but also one incredibly risky. Her responsibility laid bare her whole self and forced her to give up everything.

Fearless Mary—destined to be seen in her community as unfaithful to Joseph. She didn't allow the fear of others' opinions to affect her obedience.

Indomitable Mary—who relinquished her security, choosing the unknown of what was to come. She was aware that she could be stoned for what her neighbors and family thought she had done. The first human prepared to die for Jesus, before he was even born.

The night she pledged her service to the King of Glory—the night she agreed to the blessed yet rugged life—she said yes to things she couldn't imagine. She would need supernatural courage to walk through them. And though she was considered favored and blessed by God, he allowed her to endure the unimaginable.

Mary, favored and blessed, fled a murderous king

in the night to protect her treasure, our treasure. Mary, favored and blessed, endured losing her twelve-year-old son while on a trip to Jerusalem. She anxiously, frantically searched for her firstborn. And Mary, favored and blessed, was destined to watch her precious God-man son—the one she made room for in her young womb, the one she nursed in the night, whose fever she felt with a mother's kiss, whose tears she dried, whose skinned knees she bandaged—endure torture and shame. Mary, favored and blessed, watched as her boy hung on the cross, consumed in excruciating pain. Mary, favored and blessed, heard his familiar voice as he cried out, "My God, my God, why have you forsaken me?" Mary, favored and blessed, hung her head and slowly turned toward home as they laid him in the ground—rolling the stone firmly over all her hopes.

Mary lived a lionhearted life. From the harrowing adventure beginning with celestial greetings, to the tedious years of Jesus' boyhood, she fearlessly served God. Mary's life—it wasn't glamorous, it wasn't comfortable, it wasn't conventional or even safe, but it was blessed. The Mary I know was audaciously willing to be a vital part of the narrative, the grand story culminating in flesh. Regardless of the scary parts, regardless of the fear. And she did it with her eyes ever fixed on the God to whom she said yes.

Mary's life makes me rethink what it means to be

favored and blessed. She causes me to adjust my perspective on fear. She shows me what to do with it, how to handle it. And Mary's life encourages me to no longer see mine as tragic and unfortunate, but rather as favored and blessed. Her company reveals how stunning bravery looks on a woman, how being clothed in strength is utterly becoming.

When we search the Word and read of historical heroines, and even when we step back and look at ourselves with open eyes, we see how God is ever working. We experience the tough times, yes—the hardship, ugly crying, confusion, and trouble—but with courage we are able to say by faith that we trust him. We will go where he leads. We look up and know that though things might not be going according to our own plans, there is a much richer one in place, put there by the Master Planner.

It's up to us. We decide if we are to hold on to disappointments. We can let fear creep and grow like pond scum, reaching to our exterior and crowding out the light, or we can walk in the strength he supplies, exchanging the despicable for the dependable. We decide if we are willing to laugh without fear.

Eight

THE BEST "ME TOO"

Britt had a dream one night a few weeks before we left for Israel, just after Daisy's third diagnosis. He dreamed we were in a city but simultaneously on a beach, and we were there to help plant a church. In the dream, as he was fretting over the conditions of the dilapidated house where we were going to live, he suddenly realized he was supposed to be running a marathon at that moment. He looked down and realized he never packed his running shoes, only his slippers, which he was wearing. Right then, Daisy came galloping up on a white horse, strong and fierce. She brought the horse to a dramatic halt and said, with that spicy, intense, somewhat scolding voice she reserved for her beloved dad, "Daddy! You missed the race because of peeling paint!" She then whipped her horse around and, with power and vigor, rode regally off into the distance.

We didn't know what to do with that dream, and so questions flew back and forth between us in the safety of darkness, tucked under the duvet. Did it mean Daisy would be healed in Israel? Was the dream's city by the sea even in Israel? It looked an awful lot like Tel Aviv, where Daisy would receive her treatment. But maybe it was Boston? (We were helping to plant a church in Boston during that time.) Daisy was obviously strong and well in the dream, so was this God promising her healing? And what was this race she was talking about?

Every piece of my flesh wanted to grab on and say this was a promise of healing. But in my spirit and in Britt's spirit we knew that we would have to take it at face value and learn from it. So Britt packed his running shoes for our trip. And you know what? While we were in Israel, he ran several times a week. Sometimes, when things were really dicey, when the fear and stress got to nearly unbearable levels, he would run twice a day. On trails in the wilderness of Carmel, he went seeking God, crying out in anguished communion with him. He ran, sweat pouring like prayers, evaporating into the sharp dryness of the air.

And I ran too. Feet pounding on red soil, uneven and rustic. I ran ancient trails through ruins, roads once traveled by sandal-wearing sojourners. Roads Jesus may have walked with his disciples, joking and tossing rocks, sharing grains of wheat threshed between suntanned hands. He was there two thousand years ago, and he was there with us then.

God met us in that physical wilderness of scrubby bushes, olive trees, and jackal trails. And he met us in the emotional wilderness. He was silent, never giving answers, never promising healing, but he was there. Individually we spent hours praying, lamenting, begging. On those trails we wept; we beat our fists into the earth.

We were helpless and honest. And though we didn't get answers, though we didn't go home with the race-winning first prize of a cure for cancer, we drew nearer than ever before to Jesus—no strings attached. And we were grateful. As strange as it was, that dream ended up being a gift. It was encouraging. It was rebuking. It was a teaching moment. It was not necessarily the promise we had been looking for, and it carried no answer to our biggest concern, but it led the way to unexpected blessing.

Now, I don't think that time we spent in Israel's wilderness was the only race Daisy meant in the dream. In Hebrews 12, we are encouraged to run the race God set out for us with endurance, but her race was the one imminently before us. And we listened. She went to heaven mere months after that dream, but we still talk about it even today, willing yet to be open to what God has for us through it.

What a heartrending experience it was, though, listening to God speak but not hearing the one answer we were seeking. In my heart of hearts, I know it was best for us in the end not to know the outcome of the race for Daisy's life. We were in the early process of learning that God's love is not measured in circumstances, that listening to God and being listened to was deep, deep real love in and of itself. And it's far more valuable than answers, because while we humans tend to be goal oriented, God himself is the goal.

I know that he heard us, that he saw us, and that

brought comfort. The way he heard and saw Hagar in the wilderness as she nursed her emotional wounds after a massive catfight. Her pregnancy had caused her to feel privileged and bratty, so she behaved contemptuously toward Sarah. This led to Sarah treating Hagar so harshly that she fled, alone and pregnant with a child not really her own. Mercifully the angel of the Lord saw her and called out to her as she sat by a spring, defeated and depressed.

A restorative river, he washed over her weary soul with encouragement, promises tailor-made for her. He promised this burned-out servant woman she would have more descendants than she could count. What a tremendous thing to hear—the greatest promise women of that culture and time period could have hoped for. But what really moved Hagar—a slave carrying the child of her master, traveling in a strange land far away from all things familiar, wandering without a family to comfort her or a place to feel like she really belonged—was being noticed by God.

Hagar was in wonder over being seen, so much so that she named the well where she was in the wilderness Beer-lahai-roi: "Well of the Living One who sees me." She wasn't let off the hook in her hardship; her circumstances didn't change. No, the angel of the Lord told Hagar to go back to her mistress and submit to her. But first, he saw her. He spoke his promises to her and loved her, regardless of what had led her to that moment.

Sometimes all it takes to continue on through the valley of the shadow of death is to know God is with us—tender, loving eyes on us with every step.

A few weeks before we left for Israel my dear friend Nina shared a vision she'd had with me. She had seen me walking through the canyon where I live, on a bridge to an unknown place. I was with Britt, Isaiah, and Daisy, and Jesus was walking alongside us, watching me specifically, a look of anguish on his face. Strange red balls were being lobbed at us, but I was the one taking the brunt of it. I was absorbing the most pain, the biggest hits. And even though Jesus was right there with us, he didn't stop what was happening. He allowed whatever was causing the pain to continue, but he also remained by our side.

The vision was one of sadness, but it also birthed a sense of wonder. To know that Jesus was with us—to see his pain because of our pain—to know that he was sympathizing with me, was an unbelievably intimate thought. It awakened me anew to his loving faithfulness.

This vision ended up being somewhat of an epiphany for me, and I understand it more in retrospect than I did right then. My journey following Daisy's loss has been up and down, stop and go. There have been moments when I've found pockets of fresh insight and peace that strengthen, but then when I least expect it, I happen upon moments of rude awakening. Jesus is taking me a bit further, showing me the deeper veins of my soul.

Recently, I was reminded of Nina's vision again

when the Holy Spirit pointed out a salient biblical truth I had been ignoring. I had been seeking freedom from the bitterness that had taken root in my heart, but I had slammed right into a roadblock, a stalwart barricade. God had taken me far, but there was yet another hill to climb. It would have been impossible without the strength he offered. It was time for another heart surgery.

Hearing whispers of the Holy Spirit and knowing there was something more brewing in me that needed to be revealed and rooted out, I planned some alone time with God—alone in a theater filled with several thousand at a worship conference. I went with trepidation, fearful that I might not hear from him. I was exhausted from keeping a choke hold on things I wasn't brave enough to let go, and my heart was afraid that silence would surround me when I finally did. So that first night I held back. I couldn't worship freely, couldn't fight my way past what was welling up in me. He was about to call me out.

As I struggled defensively to sing the words, my fists balled up tighter and tighter. I stood there feeling irritable then indignant. I was mad at the world; I was mad at Satan; I was mad at every false preaching on healing and prosperity that jacks people up. And I realized I was mad at God for not healing Daisy. I had been carrying this for a long time, completely unaware. I thought that the bitterness in me was directed elsewhere, at circumstances or at hurtful people, but ultimately—I realized—I had bitterness against God.

In the theater that night, I was finally honest before the Lord. Like Job, after thirty-seven chapters of questions and laments, I felt spent. Like Job, I repented. And like Job, I finally listened to what God had to say to me, and it came as a surprise. He told me I was withholding love from him, that I was letting injustice, grudges, distrust, and anger create a barrier between us. Once it was all out on the table, I could finally begin to fully trust God, to worship unrestrained. The tears fell freely, a salty rain mingling with the tears of my friend as we prayed together, cried loud and long together, and did the arduous work of repentance, of intercession, of surrender. In that theater with the lights down low, the worship rising up, the splashing on the ground of the shared flow of human anguish mixed with love and respect, I experienced a little more healing. A little more release.

You see, before that night, I had found comfort in the difficult lives of suffering faith heroes. I had found community with them. But deep inside me was the idea that Jesus was sitting in heaven, detached from my pain, thinking, "Sucks to be you." I had forgotten that his love for me included his suffering *with* me, that he had walked with me on that bridge, felt my pain, locked his eyes with mine.

Over the next two days through personal time in the Word and times of worship, Jesus met me. He tore my walls down with truth, with wholehearted love. During the last night, as the conference was wrapping up, I received the kindest gift.

As I began to worship and open my heart again, this time a little wider, I saw him. Jesus held my face in his hands, staring fervently into my eyes. And what he said I'll never forget:

"Look at me!"

He said it again. "Look at me!"

Without letting me go, with increasing passion, he said it a last time: "Look at me!"

In that moment, in that brief vision, I was made aware that I had been looking at so many other things, so many lesser things, when I should have been looking at Jesus. I missed the fact that he was right there with me and had never left. I had been wrong about his detachment from my suffering. So very wrong.

And so I surrendered. I surrendered the idea that I can play God and control the outcome of my life. I surrendered the sinful attitudes, the self-pity, the ugly fits. I surrendered the kicking of feet and lashing out at the One who is carrying me. I surrendered the wasting of time, sitting around paralyzed because I can't get past the mess my life has become or the disappointments I have suffered. I surrendered what I had been holding back, all the love and adoration I had been withholding from God out of a broken heart: stingy, petulant, and hoarding affection.

Isaiah 63:9 says, "In all their suffering *he also suffered*" (emphasis mine). I had forgotten. I had forgotten that he wept, that he cried out in anguish, that the Man of Sorrows was deeply acquainted with suffering. Not only his own, but mine. He knows all suffering—that of the downcast, the burdened, the oppressed. I had forgotten that "since he himself has gone through suffering and testing, he is able to help us when we are being tested" (Heb. 2:18). I had forgotten that God the Father had also endured the scourge and death of his own beloved child.

When I looked at him, I heard him say, "I know, Kate. Me too."

Me too! And the hope arises, the trust increases, the love grows. The "me too" of the God-man is even better than the "me too" of my biblical sisters. It's the ultimate "me too."

He sees me. He sees you—but only when we tear our eyes away from our distractions long enough to focus will we recognize him. If we open the Book with open hearts, if we give our attention to the One who saw Hagar, the One who saw Sarah, the One who saw Daisy, the One who sees you, and the One who sees me, we can be made stronger. That truth changed me. It is making me as sure-footed as a deer, able to tread upon the heights.

Jesus said to us, "I will be with you always." The same Jesus who was in the beginning, the same Jesus who snuggled into Mary's robe to keep warm, skinned his knees, memorized the Torah, and loved the unlovely. He's the same Jesus who lifted the head of the adulterous woman, who walked on water, who hung on a cross and died a criminal's death. The same Jesus who told us to pack running shoes runs the race beside us. Jesus pours out truth and makes himself available then waits for an opportunity to have compassion on us. The same Jesus who suffers when we suffer. The best "me too."

Nine

REAL-LIFE INTERLUDE

If I were a smoker, this is where I would take a long, slow drag deep into every last alveolus. While leaning back in my wingback chair with eyes narrowed, I would tilt my head ever so slightly to let the smoke curl out of my mouth and waft unhurriedly to the ceiling, where it would assimilate into a protective haze. And as the memories trickled from the depths of a heart that's been layered and toughened by sadness and disappointment, I would lean in close to the computer, face lit only by the screen. Needful to release what is pressed down, I would thrust the smoldering symbol of hard knocks hastily back into my mouth, allowing it to dangle precariously from the lower right corner of my lips. The words would flow through my fingers, vehemently banging away at the keyboard, reliving what again landed me at the junction between disappointment and life-giving truth.

But I'm not a smoker. I'm just a girl lying in her bed, surrounded by chocolate to settle unstable nerves, with nothing to cloak my hardness but a telltale pile of tissues.

Halfway through writing this book, I experienced a miscarriage. More accurately, as I write this, I am still experiencing a miscarriage. There is nothing like sitting, waiting in sorrow for the child who was once alive inside of you to pass through, to exit your life forever. In miscarriage you get all the pain, all the discomfort of pregnancy and early labor, yet none of the reward. You are left with a first trimester muffin top and cramps that last for weeks. I told my husband this morning that miscarriage is a gyp.

Last Sunday I was preparing dinner for a couple of missionaries from Thailand and some dear friends who are also on staff at our church. It was a gorgeous summer afternoon, and the ranch was perfect. Our iceberg roses were in bloom and bountiful, the patio freshly swept and free of eucalyptus leaves. There was food on platters to be enjoyed at leisure. We had just gotten our pigs, so they were still small and cute, running around in their pen, making for comically sweet scenery. I had made a tasty sauce for the fish my father-in-law had caught, and we were barbecuing them for dinner. Life—so beautiful, so full of flavor and promise. Baby in my belly, friends, love, beauty, hope.

Then I felt it. That twinge in your body that says something's not right. Early on in the evening I went to the bathroom and saw pink. Not bright red but pink, so there was hope, right? What should have been a lovely evening was, for me, full of secret apprehension. How quickly the tides change. It was like in the movies when all of a sudden the sky turns black and rain comes down in sheets though it had been sunshine and rainbows the minute before, but this time without the fun of making out under a makeshift shelter with the leading man. Snap. So fast.

The next day I paid a visit to my dear OB-GYN, whom I have seen the last eighteen years. I purposely wore no perfume. Have you ever noticed how connected scent and memory are? The right whiff can take me back to the beach where I grew up as a kid, or to my seventh-grade year and it feels like I have a perm again. I've learned that I don't want to have a scent attached to days that might bring bad news. I don't want any smell connected to the memory of a professional in a white coat telling me whether my child will live or die.

And so I went, unscented, and climbed up on that table with its pseudo-recliner angle and its unrolled paper to protect it from any unsavory emissions from my body. That thin, almost waxy paper crinkled conspicuously underneath me as I shifted in discomfort, as the doctor probed for signs of life in my womb. I read the truth on his face. Silence in the cold room with the charts of female anatomy, with the women's interest magazines and drawers of various pads and cloths and packaged cleansing wipes. Silence that made me wish I had shaved my legs, bent awkwardly in those wretched stirrups. Silence that says there has been another death in my family, another heart ripped from my own. Another reason to shed tears, another reason to have to look my husband and son in the eyes and shake my head, saying, "No. No dice."

Breathe.

He showed me the screen, how there was no life. He said, "This is not normal. I'm so sorry. Would you like some medicine to hurry along the inevitable?"

Medicine to pass what was left of my fifth child onto cotton pads, into the septic system. He said it would likely make me vomit and would be quite painful, so I declined. I had to wait for the nurse to give me a RhoGAM shot as my blood was RH negative, and the three minutes it took was like plugging a dam with my index finger. I was going to burst at any moment.

Hold on, hold on . . .

She looked me in the eye and said she was sorry, that it was sad. But you know, I've done so much mourning with strangers over the years that I felt I needed to keep these tears to myself. Needed to let God collect them in his bottle. Needed to share them with only my husband and teenage son.

So I looked away and compartmentalized.

It was fine, I told her. I would be fine. At least I wasn't as far along as last time, nervous chuckle. *Just give me the shot, lady, so I can drive and cry and pray I don't crash.*

All week I have been in pain. Last time I had a miscarriage eleven years ago I went in for a D&C, so I have never experienced the drawn-out natural version. This version leaves you sick and with ruined underwear. A constant reminder that life is rude—that a broken world takes love, takes life from a mother's body, and flushes it down the toilet. A reminder that there is nothing I can do to save this child. There was nothing I could do to save Daisy's life, or the life of my second baby. I am sick with the thought that I have lost.

I lost the contest; I lost the race. I couldn't do it, couldn't make them survive. Only two of my children walk the earth. Only two of them are around to give and receive hugs and ice cream and prayers and corrections. Only two left. My family is like a jack-o'-lantern missing most of its teeth, its kooky smile showing its deficit.

So I sit in my bed, surrounded by a jar of chocolate chips, a banana, and cashew butter, acutely aware that not all is right in the world. It may never be. There is no better time to face another heartbreak than in the middle of writing about how great the future is, how with strength and dignity I can walk through anything. There is no better time than now to face Jesus and adjust my perspective, to view my surroundings accordingly.

I need truth. I need it when I read about the speakers at an upcoming conference who all have four to seven children, and when I feel overcome with jealousy at the pictures of beautiful people surrounded with beautiful children piled up like puppies in hipster pickup trucks. I need truth when the fear of loving anyone new creeps up, because they might just leave me and die. I need truth when I wonder if it's safer to detach, safer when there are fewer people to love. I need truth when the sharp tang of depression flavors my thoughts—*I knew it, I knew that would happen. Why is it me, always me? Why does death follow me around like a gross stray dog who pees foul yellow on every bright flower, every growing and flourishing thing?*

Whenever we lose a child I feel just that—like a loser. I get this lame feeling, like I wasn't good enough, couldn't make the cut. When you've wanted something so badly you could taste it, when you've dreamed and named and pictured the way your future would look and it's gone in a moment, wiped away with one ultrasound, you feel lost. When you've been so excited to give a baby to the family, to grow them all a gift. When you've hoped beyond all hope you could give the thumbs-up to the people who have prayed for you and supported you and cheered you on, and you have to face them and tell them their hopes were dashed along with yours.

Funny how it's not my grown-out roots that make me feel like a loser (I was waiting until after first trimester to see my hairstylist), or the flannel shirt unbuttoned over an ill-fitting, dirty T-shirt. It's not the saggy PJ bottoms or the spilled jar of chocolate chips or the mounting pile of dishes. It's the dashed hopes, the letdown felt with every cramp, with the bleeding of hope.

Life can be sad. Incredibly sad. Like how-many-weeks-has-it-been-since-my-mascara-stayed-on-past-nine-a.m. sad. We are created as emotional beings complete with tear ducts, noses that run, and red faces that betray our true feelings. You know, even Jesus wept, and that is a comfort to me. There is a time to mourn.

Nothing stays the same. Nothing. Children grow up and people change. Church communities ebb and flow; hopes rise and fall. Marriages grow and weaken; some break up. Career paths and moves and family emergencies all paint our lives with different colors. Some are solemn and some are vibrant. For Pete's sake, even my rear end has changed, traveled south—and she's not coming back up where she belongs anytime soon, if ever.

So I drink in truth. I drink in the only life that is sure, the very Word of God. What was that he said? Remind me, for I can't see through the muddle of tears, the feeling of rejection, the shaking in fear.

If I idolize a certain season of life, I will drown. I must learn to extract the joy from each and every season, or I will experience a different kind of death. I can't live in the past; I can't live in a place of missing the good old days. I need to agree with Jesus that, while things can be different or even disappointing, there is still a life abundant for me to grab hold of.

And now I know—after sitting for a while and mourning the baby we won't meet until eternity, after doing the math and despising how we only have two of five children alive on earth, after the wiping of tears and the smearing of mascara, and after explaining to my family that they, too, have lost another member—I look up.

I surrender my hopes for what I wanted my family to look like, sacredly giving it to the Lord. I accept what he has chosen for us; I believe that he loves us. I look around and thank him for his generosity. I hug the baby a bit more, feeling her chubby face on my thinning one. I laugh with my fourteen-year-old son when he tells me funny stories of his friends and their crushes and how many waves he caught that day. I choose to be swallowed up in my tall, strong husband's firm embrace, to bury my face in his barrel chest, grateful that we don't face death alone.

I have so much.

Ten

JUST A LITTLE BIT OF POOP

Okay, friends. I just want to take a quick time-out to acknowledge this apparent obsession I have with bathroom topics and references. For that, I'm sorry. As I ponder the inappropriately proportioned number of poop mentions I insist upon including, I realize that for far too long in my household, the only people I've had to talk to who can respond in language I understand are a teenage boy and his father—the latter of whom has informed me that, no, men never grow out of bathroom humor no matter how mature/successful/godly/influential they become. Yes, he says, it's still hilarious. With this sage wisdom in mind, I bring you this chapter. I apologize to my female readers who live without a male under their roof. Poop happens.

I have this friend named Kelly. She is effortlessly beautiful, has five gorgeous kids, is laid back and cool, loves Jesus, and pretty much doesn't sin. She loves the Word, old saints, spiritual heavyweight books, and she'll preach your face off. She holds the line at home, where there are always forty-two extra kids running around, and she has the patience of Mr. Miyagi. She also has freckles and talks with her hands, so she gets extra points.

I was at the beach with her one day several years ago, sometime near the beginning of Daisy's cancer treatment. Her youngest daughter, whom they had adopted recently, was playing on a blanket while our sons surfed. Said youngest daughter had a dirty diaper, and, as moms do, Kelly changed it on the blanket we were all sitting on without missing a beat in our conversation. Wham bam.

One of her boys had gotten out of the water by that time and came to sit down on the blanket for a snack. He realized there was a remaining smear of poop on one corner. Not a huge chunk—merely a smallish knob, but still, supergross. Kelly's son vocalized what I was keeping inside (because I'm a grown-up and have learned that, unlike Shakespeare's Rosalind, though I am a woman, when I think, I must not always speak).

"Ew, Mom, that's so gross! Mom, the poop! There's poop on the blanket! Gross, Mom!" He started making gagging noises and was writhing in exaggerated yet appropriately dramatized disgust. He was freaking out over the caca on the blanket, and—sorry, Kelly—I was right there with him in spirit.

Kelly, a teensy bit older but a heap wiser than I, waved it off with a flutter and said in her blasé way, "It's fiiiiiine. You're fiiiiiine. It's just a little bit of poop"—as if there was absolutely nothing to worry about and her son was absurd for even pointing it out.

And since then, no eleven words have helped me more. Honestly. You see, Kelly has lived some life. She has a passel of kids, is a pastor's wife, has endured tough changes in ministry, moving, loss of loved ones, and has foster-parented kids with a range of emotional and behavioral difficulties. She has been a faithful follower of Jesus, living a real, un-photoshopped life, and she knows what is and isn't worth worrying about.

Sure, poop is gross. But in the grand scheme, that's all it is. Just a little bit of poop.

Since that day, my husband and I have used that phrase countless times. Traffic on LA freeways on the way to the hospital? Just a little bit of poop. Spilled coffee on the couch? Just a little bit of poop. Toddler with a hair-pulling problem, rendered completely bald on top? Just a little bit of poop. Basically, if it's not cancer, it's just a little bit of poop.

Just last spring the four of us went on vacation to Hawaii. As part of a surfboard-making family, and having had the privilege of walking alongside our dear friends who planted a church there, we know and love the north shore of Oahu. It's the ideal place for relaxation, and it's filled with Hawaiian family and great surf. The way the untamed Pacific meets the shore, wild and translucent, breeding life and warmth and the heady scent of salt and plumeria, makes it my favorite earthly indulgence. It's a soul-healing place to be.

The second night of our twelve-night stay, we took

some friends out to dinner at a lovely restaurant on a golf course. Palms swaying, tans glowing, laughter pealing out between our two families who love one another so, we basked in the sweet knowing that comes with having served Jesus in the trenches together. It was a gorgeous evening with incredible food and lots of love.

Right when our much-anticipated dinners showed up, Fifi demanded to be taken out of her nylon high chair and to sit on Daddy's lap. Britt is a softy and, this being child number three (we'd thrown so much discipline out the window by that time), he immediately acquiesced to her wishes. Not fifteen seconds went by before he noticed warmth and a smear on the upper thigh of his corduroy pants. A big, juicy, chunky, pungent smear, deep in the wales of his thankfully already brown pants. As he had picked her up, wanting to quickly get back to his hot dinner, he'd failed to notice that Fifi had had a significant bout of diarrhea in her high chair. Not only had it filled the hammock-like seat to the brim, but it had also soaked her dress and christened Britt. Soon the poop was all over both of our arms, splattered in forlorn piles on the floor, and stinking up what was supposed to be a picturesque sunset dinner with friends.

We quickly moved the baby to the grass of the golf course to tackle the situation. Out came the wipes, which methodically multiplied themselves like embryonic cell division. We promptly were surrounded by piles and piles of soiled, wadded-up casualties of war. Once Fifi was clean, I walked back to my seat bent over, slowly snaking through the tables looking for poop splatters like Sherlock Holmes looking for clues. Here and there I kneeled down by other diners' sarong-covered sunburned knees to swiftly make a sludgy land mine disappear. Nothing to see here, folks.

After much water, enough wipes to make a significant carbon footprint, a quick change into a spare dress for the baby, and trying our hardest to endure the scent, sight, and very thought of Britt's poopy pant leg, we cut our losses and tapped out. I gulped down my warm bacon spinach salad, the boys inhaled their coconut shrimp, and we called it a night.

Pulling into our friend's house where we were staying, I was mildly irritated. Okay, Isaiah informed me I was snapping. All I had wanted was to enjoy a nice dinner for once, one that someone else had prepared. Was that too much to ask? Instead, right on the heels of our "fun" dinner, I was hunched over in the dark, desperately spraying off the sloppy, soaked high chair, scraping stubborn bits with my nail, muttering to myself about the situation like a madwoman.

Elbow deep in muck, my phone rang. Caller ID said it was our friend who was staying at our house while we were gone. She was a darling girl, full of joy and grace, and there existed a heart connection between us, two people who have lost dear loves. (Her brother had died in a diving accident a bit before Daisy.) She had been couch surfing and camping out for several weeks because her house had been flooded by a broken pipe, so we extended an invitation for her to have a solid place to stay for the twelve days we were gone. We wanted to give the poor girl some rest and a place to relax.

Normally, I would have loved to see her name on my screen, but on this night, I knew it wasn't a good thing.

"Hello?"

Shaky, labored breathing.

"Are you okay?"

In a tremulous voice she said, "I'm okay. I'm okay."

My imagination automatically ran wild. I pictured bandits holding her at gunpoint, feral and unshaven, pithy arrogance and spittle flying as they rudely disregarded her repeated pleas to get lost. I frantically asked what happened, feeling horrible about putting her in a place of danger, out in the country where our house isn't close to neighbors, where it would take the police too long to arrive. I imagined her lying there bleeding, waiting for the ambulance to make its way up our windy road, her shoulder shot through by the leader of the dastardly pack.

But you know what actually happened? She had started rinsing a garment in our utility sink, gotten distracted, and left the faucet running while she went out to dinner. When she came back to our house later on, her heart sank as she immediately heard the telltale trickle of water spilling onto the wood floor. The utility sink had no drain on the side, only in the bottom; but she had plugged that one up and, therefore, unintentionally flooded my house. Actually, really, she flooded my laundry room, bedroom, and closet. But, yeah, there was a flood. The second one for her in a matter of weeks.

By the time she had gotten hold of me there was an entire cleanup crew in my bedroom. They were packing my things, sucking up water, and going hard after the damage. Within hours my entire personal life was in a storage container in my driveway, everything labeled accordingly: framed pictures, baby clothes, books, shoes.

Minutes earlier, I had been grumbling about some poop on a twenty-dollar high chair, completely missing that we were on a Hawaiian vacation. At a terrific restaurant with people we loved. And now I was receiving this news. Should I have erupted over the accidental flooding of my bedroom, oblivious to the fact that we had insurance? That the damage was covered? That it was being taken care of and all my pretty things were safe and out of harm's way? The choice was obvious. It was time to adjust my view, to see things for what they really were. A little bit of poop among a world of blessing.

Britt and I have walked through a lot of poop together. Literally—baby poop, horse poop, pig poop, dog poop, chicken poop—and figuratively—ministry trials and house flooding, for starters. What we've learned through it all is that when you look at life and realize poop happens, well, you know that it washes off.

Some things can't be washed off. Instead they wound and scar and leave you limping—like cancer, infidelity, or abuse. But the things that can be washed off? Don't give them a second thought, because they don't deserve it. Don't miss the race because of peeling paint.

Perspective is a gift. It can save lives, alerting us to imminent danger, and it can keep us safe too. With perspective we can walk in confidence on an otherwise unsteady pathway. Without perspective, we can't drive or walk. We wouldn't be able to see properly—gauge size or distance—or experience the fullness of beauty. We may think we can see clearly, but without perspective we will miss important details.

It's kind of like when Owl from *Winnie the Pooh and the Blustery Day* says, "Chin up, and all that sort of thing." Eeyore could argue that we need to see it all, that we cannot ignore the darkness that seems ever present. He might say that happiness is fake and we just need to be honest about all the ways life sucks. After all, who's kidding whom? Tigger is annoying.

I have spent some time being Eeyore, with his "realistic," tell-it-like-it-is persona, and I have found that ultimately this mind-set doesn't glorify God. Nor does it take into account the whole picture, the whole truth. It minimizes the goodness, provision, and plans of God that we may not see at the moment. But when we step back to consider the full scope of the story, putting things into perspective, we magnify God's gifts and end up practicing gratitude. This does not diminish the reality of tough times, but it does open our hearts to acknowledge what God has done and is still doing.

The apostle Paul knew of what he spoke when he reminded us to give thanks in every situation, offered along with our petitions. There are needs and hardships, and he acknowledged them. But he also prescribed the way through the need, the trouble, the affliction: thankfulness.

So often when Daisy's health and treatment got really hairy, Britt and I would comfort one another by casting light on what was true and lovely. When we spent our days and nights under the artificial lights of a hospital room and were surrounded by the cacophony of flashing and beeping machines, we reminded ourselves that we were blessed to have access to treatment. When the days dragged on, when the small square of sunlight crept past the solid stucco wall that was our only view, we thought how fortunate we were that I didn't have to go to work and could spend every moment with Daisy. That perspective turned a wretched situation into a cherished opportunity to snuggle and bond more deeply.

Every time we sat in a stark, generic conference room and received life-altering news over a Formica table, or systematically were informed of all the side effects our girl would likely experience, or learned that she would be infertile, that she couldn't withstand a stem cell transplant, and that she was going to die . . . we felt so thankful that we weren't single parents. We were grateful to share the brunt of the whole horrifying affair, to cry in each other's arms, and glad to be a team that could not be broken.

I hope all this glossy gratitude doesn't sound trite or smug or overly pious to you. Telling God what we needed while thanking him for what we had was a hard-won endeavor, one fought on the battlefield of tears, confusion, and utter terror. And while I also realize I had more to be thankful for than some in our situation—a solid spouse, abundant support, and a flexible schedule—the struggle was real. It was not an automatic response to our situation, not something we didn't labor to believe. It wasn't something that once we figured out how to navigate, we automatically went back to, but something that was a fight each and every time—especially after Daisy breathed her last and we found ourselves on a completely different battlefield. But the victory was sweet. Since Daisy died, I've relearned to see the bright spots through the shadows. I've walked in remembrance, teaching myself all over again to be anxious for nothing, to pray for what I need with thanksgiving, to open my hands freely to what may fall into them, even while someone precious had fallen out of them.

Wouldn't you know it, after I poured out the sadness into the Lord's hands and set my face on what was true and good and lovely, I grew stronger. I had strength to get out of bed in the morning. Strength to survive the emotional holocaust of the suffering and death of a child.

Strength to honor God in worship, to love well those whom God has placed around me. And true to what Paul said in chapter 4 of his letter to the Philippians, so came the peace washing over me, softly covering the skin of my soul like a balm, guarding my heart and mind in Christ Jesus.

We all know how capable we are of seeing the one thing we don't have and becoming fixated on how we can't possibly live without it. Whatever it is—healing or babies or love—it beckons like a siren call. *I want it now.* But if we look up from our daze of desire, if we stop and think for a second, we all know where that got Eve. When we think of Eve, we get all judgy and want to say, "Really, Eve? The one thing that wasn't yours for the taking in the entire garden? How could you not see how ridiculous that was?" We shake our heads and roll our eyes and blame our menstrual cramps on her. But we are Eve. Every. Single. Day.

As a culture, as Westerners, we are blind. We are blind to blessing and blind to wisdom. We want the thing we don't have. We want perfect triceps and shapely calves. We want homes that sparkle and grace the pages of a magazine. We want ant-free picnics, cloud-free beach days. We want someone else's marriage, someone else's life. And we want piles and piles of the shiny things we are convinced will make us happy.

It reminds me of my son, Isaiah. He was talking to one of the nurses at the clinic in Israel while we were there receiving treatment for Daisy. He was almost twelve at the time and had a miles-long list of gifts he hoped to receive for his upcoming birthday. Legos, mostly. He showed her the list and, dumbfounded, she said, "I can't imagine ever giving someone a list of presents I want them to buy me!" She shook her head in astonishment and dubiously questioned me about such crazy talk.

It might seem a bit odd to those of us who grew up in the US that she's never even thought about making a wish list, but you know what? She's not the one whose perspective is off. Ours is.

Our hunger for more, better, sparklier will never be satisfied. We are the children who, surrounded by mounds of unnecessary and excessive articles of diversion on Christmas morning, say, "Is that it?" I'm talking to myself right now and all of Western civilization. More is not always more. Let the scales fall from our eyes so we can see the abundance that is already ours. The joys we don't even consider, the pleasures we disregard. We take for granted our families, gifts, and abilities, and we fail to remember how we don't deserve a thing, not even the breath in our lungs. All is the grace of a generous Father.

Whatever happened to reveling in the joy of holding your baby? Of being able to throw her up in the air and catch her on the way down as her curls lift and sway in the wind? What about the honor and privilege of carrying a child in your womb, the way every outgrown article of clothing is a sign of your baby's good health? How

about feeling spent after belly laughter at a bonfire, singing your lungs out at church, or sticking your head out
the window while flying down a tree-lined street? And
what about the feeling of sand between your toes, the
simple thrill of your best friend sitting on the handle-
bars of your bicycle, or a tart lemonade on a hot day?
The scent of sunshine on a sprawling tomato vine, the
way clean sheets feel against freshly showered skin? The
icy cold flesh of a dewy sweet watermelon, the sound of
breaking suction when a toddler pulls her thumb out of
her mouth in order to hug you? What about the sensation
of a contented sigh, or the sight of a child smiling wide,
showcasing the gap of her first lost tooth? My point is, we
have way more than we realize. Our lives are abundant,
overflowing with beauty we often overlook. Don't miss it.

A few days ago I was in my husband's study at around
6:30 a.m. He rises at four a.m. every day to study and
pray, and when the baby wakes I like to take her in there
and lounge on the couch for a minute while she climbs on
his lap. She gives him morning-breath kisses and sucks
the ink out of his highlighter markers. That morning I
had gotten up at five to write and wanted to read to him
what I had written. I not only wanted to read it to him
but also wanted him to adequately feel the gravity of it—
to narrow his eyes and nod slowly, to let out an "Mmm,"

perhaps do a light fist pound over his heart. And then I wanted him to kiss me and tell me I was brilliant. This is important stuff.

A sentence or two into my satisfyingly dramatic homily, Fifi started to babble and talk. Really loudly. It would have been so cute except she was drowning me out and completely ruining the moment. And since it's all about me, I stopped and rolled my eyes and hushed her. And you know what Britt said to me?

"She's alive."

That's it. Those two words, just like, "It's fine, you're fine, just a little bit of poop"—they pack so much freedom for me. It's a silly illustration, I know, but the perspective it affords is not a bit silly. She's alive! My messy teenager who left the hose running for two days straight? He's alive! My husband whose hunting obsession leaves me for days on end with a two-year-old and a looming deadline? He's alive! And suddenly, at the fork in the road, where you can either turn toward pity or party, well, break out the streamers because there are people to be loved and thanks to be given.

Perspective is a giver. Comparison takes. Perspective is generous. Comparison pares down the loveliness of your life until it appears a thin shred of its former glory. Perspective carries us through life laughing. Comparison evokes cursing and frowns and grumbling.

Perspective says that I got eight years with the dearest little fairy a mama could hope for. Comparison says I got ripped off. Perspective says going to Israel was a gift to our family, the magic of extra time away together that melded us closer as a family amid every bite of hummus, every impatient honk and Hebrew profanity aimed at us, every car ride through pockmarked villages. Comparison says the three months we spent in Israel heaped hardship upon hardship, needlessly stretching paper-thin nerves. Perspective says we are blessed that Daisy didn't die in obscurity but with the support of thousands who prayed and loved and sacrificed for her, who felt our pain and remember her beauty. Comparison says I don't care if your kids learned compassion through her story; your kid is still right there with you and mine is gone.

One night in early November, just a week or so before we left Israel, Daisy and I were lying in bed together. There we were, under the thin borrowed covers, two bodies pressed into one another like spoons. Her form was so small, so spindly. Her hair was about an inch long, a fair, silky fleece she worked so hard to grow. In the stillness, we had late-night discussions of things an eight-year-old should never have to think about. And we breathed, together as one body, as if she were still in my womb, covered by my heartbeat.

We had been staying in a rental home in a hilltop town called Zikhron Ya'akov, a half Orthodox and half Gentile, good old-fashioned heathen town. We were nearing the end of our time there and Daisy didn't seem to be getting much better. We had watched the sky metamorphose from dusky tan, melting into the land without border, to a more vivid blue, dotted with clouds pregnant with the necessary elements to bring life to the earth. The dramatic clouds were bold and fierce and full of emotion, much like every sabra in Israel, much like us toward the end of our journey there. And those clouds let loose.

Thunderstorms in Israel during that time of year are breathtaking. They are loud, torrential, electrifying. As we lay in the darkness together, the room lit up. The storm was over our heads, and the decibel level was more than I'd ever experienced. The rain came in sheets through the black night, violently entering the atmosphere, piercing the cracked earth. It was the thunderstorm of thunderstorms, a display of the magnitude that is creation, contrasted with the frailty of humanity.

That night was a gift to me. The tears, the bravery of my shattered daughter, the way she melted into me—all of it a gift. I had no assurance of anything other than the God of heaven, his sovereignty, his fearsome might. And so I chose in that moment not to shrink from the lightning but to see the beauty in its potency. To not lose the magic of the moment by agonizing further about my daughter's declining health. I chose to feel the warmth between us, to see the artful images the shadows on the wall were creating, to connect with the gift that was my firstborn daughter—who was still very much alive, still able to be enjoyed.

That terrifying yet wondrous night was like so much of life. Sometimes a few smudges mess up the shiny days, but other times the most priceless gift exists smack-dab in the middle of the worst. A clarity of vision, seeing the bigger picture painted by a generous God, makes all the difference. Just as I learned all these crucial things during the fight for Daisy's life, I have learned to carry this over into my post-Daisy world of grief. It makes the sad days bearable and the average days magical. Life blooms radiant in the times I choose perspective over comparison, when I see poop for what it is and let the storm wash it clean.

Eleven

DO YOU SEE IT?

I live by the beach. Actually, I live in a funky, ghetto-chic neighborhood filled with organic vegetable farms, horse ranches, avocado ranches, and lemon ranches, just over the hill from the beach. The dwellings near me consist of everything from tiny trailers and shanties to the big mansion next door. On our property we keep pigs and chickens and the occasional horse, and the whole rest of the canyon is filled with donkeys, mini horses, full-grown horses, dogs, barn cats, and even some mules. The hawks circle endlessly, and coyotes hang around at twilight, waiting for a house cat to be let out—just in time for a feral cocktail hour.

We've even had bear sightings when the weather gets really dry. When those big furry fellas work up an awful thirst in our perpetually drought-ridden Golden State, they come out of the Los Padres National Forest to drink out of a garden hose or lounge in a pool. This doesn't have too much to do with the story I'm about to tell you, but because we're friends now I thought I'd give you a snapshot of what it's like in my world. And I like to stage a story before I get to the heart of it, as you may have noticed—so enjoy the journey, man.

So, the beach. I was driving down the Pacific Coast

Highway awhile ago with my crazy bearded husband in his giant Silverado. We were searching for waves. There are abundant great breaks up and down the coast, some popular and crowded, some secret and localized (which basically means you had better know someone who surfs there unless you want your tires slashed).

There is one particularly popular spot that is perfect for beginners, and it is always crowded. Like, jam-packed. The parking lot is a colorful medley of humanity. There are old VW vans plastered with social-consciousness stickers that suggest we question reality. There are lifted four-cylinder trucks boasting the typical Mexican beer stickers of the college bound—the proud stamp of a first surf trip across the border without your parents. There are Subarus bearing Patagonia stickers and toting rugged, adventuresome, REI-shopping thirtysomethings, and minivans crammed with piles of kids and their various flotation devices. You'll see crossovers with aging women grasping at the shadow of their athletic youth, recapturing the feeling of freedom via wave riding, and you'll also see cheap, beat-up cars with stacked surfboards sticking out the passenger windows—not enough cash flow to buy a set of surf racks. It's hilarious.

But what's even more hilarious was the man we saw in a beach chair that day. There he sat, tan and leathery, sunning his voluminous white beard in all its glory. He looked like Kris Kringle on vacay. Carbonated beverage in holder, chair back reclined. Enjoying the day and taking in the sights, breathing deeply the exhaust from the cars whizzing by mere feet from his face.

What? Yes, you heard me. The man was sitting on the side of the road, right where the cars were parked. He was facing the beach, I suppose, but the highway and a rock wall lay between him and the sand. Just about twenty-five yards farther, and this man could have dug his old brown toes gratifyingly in the sand. He could have traded toxic fumes for salty sea air. What was he thinking? So close, yet so far.

I don't know what the problem was. Perhaps he'd had some bad experiences at the beach in the past. Maybe a dog had lifted its leg on his lunch box or a seagull had pooped on his comb-over. A stray kid could have kicked sand all over his freshly laid towel, or sand crabs might have nibbled his toes. It's possible that he was afraid of sharks or stingrays or wanted to avoid the occasional dead seal decomposing at low tide and the stink associated with it. All these things were possible, or even probable. Comes with the territory.

Whatever his issue was, it got me thinking. He thought he was at the beach—but he wasn't actually at the beach. He was near the beach. With only a short walk, a bit more effort, and a pinch of resolve, his experience could have changed from mediocre (torturous, in my opinion, to not be lying leisurely in the sand) to magnificent. So often we are that guy when it comes to following Jesus. We set up camp nearby the prize, we come close to the real thing, but for whatever reason, we don't fully engage.

How often do we act satisfied in our walk with Jesus without actually going the distance? We say we follow him, we sing the songs, we show up on Sundays, but we don't engage in the scarier stuff. The costly stuff. The risky stuff. Stuff like true and unshrinking love. Serving. Teaching. Giving. Praying. Even accepting his will. We miss out on the honesty of opening up in authentic relationship, letting people see the real us. We miss out on answering God's call, on saying yes to him and his crazy ideas.

We want the blessing of a Christian life but none of the pain. We think twice about diving in, risking love because we might lose it, risking reputation, comfort, all these things we think will keep us safe and happy. We sit in a beach chair across the street because we don't want to get dirty or uncomfortable or become a target for seagulls. Well, guess what? Going all-out with Jesus will be messy! Jesus even said so himself. We will get wet and sandy and pooped on. We will get exhausted and spend time cleaning up messes, we will become war-weary. No one ever said it would be immaculate.

I got peed on at the beach this year. It was humiliating and infuriating. It was during a local surf contest my husband and son enter every year. I had spent the past two contests either bulging in pregnancy or tending a needy newborn, so this year I was enjoying the dignity of having all my parts tucked in.

This surf contest is great fun. It's a long-standing tradition. Everyone in town comes out for it, and there are so many people to catch up with. The guys lightheartedly rib each other about who will get the prize belt buckle this year and who will be the "first loser" (second place). Bags of chips travel between sand-covered kids, and naughty dogs make off with turkey sandwiches. Sunscreen gets slathered until the distinct smell hangs thick in the air, a charming reminder of our own childhoods.

I was sitting in the sand in front of the crowd near the water's edge, watching the action while deep in conversation with a friend. Almost unnoticeably, I felt a light sensation of fur on my side. And then the warmth. The pee spread down my ribs and onto my hip, thick and noxious. It was the Australian Shepherd that lives at the house there on the beach.

"Are you freaking kidding me?!" flew out of my mouth before I could stop it, and I jumped up in a rage. I saw a few people try to act like they hadn't noticed, which was kind of them. But many more did. I'm not a violent person, but in that moment I would have punched the dog in the face if he hadn't run. I stamped off the beach—irate, disgusted, pathetic.

It was a bad day, though all signs had pointed to it being a glorious one. But can you imagine all I would miss if I never went back to the beach again? If I gave up on beaches because of an unfortunate situation? Since that miserable day, I have surfed sparkling waves, built countless sand castles with Fifi, and enjoyed sun-drenched conversations with great friends. I've had the pleasure of sharing waves with my son, and I've watched my husband outsurf every guy in the lineup. Not going back to the beach because of a potential bummer is like sitting on the highway: I would be missing out on some great stuff.

If I'm sitting on the highway, if I don't cross over, I won't experience the fullness, the fierce living I was made for. But if I go back to the beach despite what happened, I will have seashells as a reminder of the beauty I breathed in there. My sore muscles will echo all the great waves I rode and the hard work it took to catch them. I will bring home the sounds of the surf crashing, the glow on my face, the spent feeling of the full experience. The truth is, I can wash off sand and dog pee. I can take a shower and get comfy in my favorite sweats, my skin still warm underneath. I can always remember the splendor of crossing over. But if I gave up and never went back, I would have none of the blessings.

I have the privilege of being close friends with some of the coolest women on the planet. Women who haven't had the easiest rides, which were either out of their control or due to their own sin. Women who have faced the disgrace of having children out of wedlock despite being raised in Christian homes, women who have endured the sorrow of carrying an infant to term who, because of a severe genetic disorder, would die mere hours later. Women who

have been faithful to husbands who are addicted to pornography. And women who have been faithful to Jesus
and his calling throughout their forty years of singleness,
when their hearts' desire is marriage. Women who have
situations in life as unglamorous as Bathsheba, as Sarah,
as me.

You know what makes these girls so cool? They
crossed over. My friend with the child out of wedlock?
She helps run an orphanage in Uganda and cares for
the cast-aside and unwanted. And by the grace of God,
she eventually married her son's father. My other friend
whose son was born while she was unmarried and barely
more than a teen? She and her baby-daddy husband
became foster parents, adopted two girls into their family
of five, and made it a family of seven. She also founded
a nonprofit benefiting foster kids and their families. The
dauntless mama who loved her infant son for eighteen
hours then handed over his body? She leads worship with
courage and pluck, heartbreaking honesty mingling with
pure love, bringing others into intimacy with Jesus by the
voice God has blessed her with. The dear one who has
chosen to love her husband through his gut-wrenching
pornography addiction? She now lovingly leads other
women down the same rough road with truth, strength,
humor, and exceptional grace. And my wonderful friend,
single at forty, who would have married twenty years ago
had she met the right man? Well, she has been a mission-
ary for the last ten years in the Middle East, sacrificially

sharing Jesus with Jews and Muslims while living a life of adventure, however uncomfortable and lonely.

Though each woman bears scars, however fresh or faint, not one has allowed her circumstances to keep her from a full life, from serving God in the sphere she has been given. Each has found real joy in the surrender. They are all beautiful, hilarious, fun, talented, and hard-working, but the bottom line is, these girls are awesome because Jesus is awesome. Through faith and because of deep love for the Savior, each has made a choice to cross over. It was not easy, but they did not stay in sadness or shame or even cling to earthly comfort. Rather, they sacrificed and believed and continue to live lives worthy of praise—just like the Proverbs 31 woman. I am honored to be surrounded by such faith and chutzpah.

I don't want to miss it. I want to cross over, to follow Jesus to the ends of the earth and right on into heaven. Sarah has followed. Bathsheba has followed. Mary has followed too. I refuse to allow grief and bitterness to keep me from following. In the face of the sand and salt and seagull poop, I say to my God, "Pick me! I'll go!" I'll risk potential pain and discomfort. I'll give up what's easy for a far more glorious life, for a life that is nowhere near perfect. I'll take a life that includes radical loss and great pain but is fully in him.

Being paralyzed with fear and sadness, being rendered useless because of bitterness, only marks a victory for the enemy of my soul. But do you know what agrees with the

Father, what shines in triumph, what brings glory to the Lord of heaven? Choosing to bring all I've learned, all the Scripture, all the words of Jesus, to the front of my life and standing on it. In him I stand and don't fall, and I live. I live for eternity.

Choosing to live for eternity is such a game changer. It holds much meaning for the future, yes, but for the here and now it brings with it the ability to laugh. A hundred years ago, when I was in college, my pastor used to say, "You *do* what you believe." He meant that we say so much—we talk, talk, talk—but what we do speaks louder. We can talk until we go hoarse, but our actions show what our faith actually looks like.

If I believe I will see Daisy again, I can grieve, but not as those without hope grieve (1 Thess. 4:13). I can cry and hurt and wail and get it all out, but I can be confident in our future reunion (1 Thess. 4:14). I can wonder joyfully about her and what she's doing. I can picture her in heaven riding a bear—or any of the crazy animals she loved so much—while eating a juicy mango, wild and free. I can see her meeting new friends and Jesus swinging her around like an airplane. I can trust she is well, she is whole, and she has done more than the things on her bucket list. I still keep that list tucked in the middle of Laura Ingalls Wilder's *On the Banks of Plum Creek*, the last book we read together, the one we never got to finish.

I believe she is with the Lord. I can rejoice in that,

and maybe, if I really think hard about it, I might even be able to laugh.

Do you see it? Hope. Confidence. Wonder. Joy. Trust. Laughter.

If I believe Jesus is the Bread of Life, the Beginning and the End, if I believe Jesus adorned himself in humanity, lived a humble life, and was scorned, tortured, and crucified to make atonement for me, will I not love him with all I've got? Will I not still follow him regardless of where my life goes, regardless of any suffering I might endure? I have decided it has been my honor and pleasure to love and serve with my whole life this God who became humble, even to death on a cross.

If I believe this life is not all there is, shouldn't I live accordingly? Will I allow despair to swallow me when I know the goodness that is coming is incomparable? If I know I will be with Jesus, face-to-face with him forever, will I not now live like a child who is well taken care of and loved by her parents? Free, joyful, secure. I believe that I will be in the presence of the Lord, and part of being ready for him is enjoying the goodness we have now. Crossing over into the fruit of belief.

If broken Bathsheba can say in Proverbs 31 that an excellent woman laughs at the future, so can I. If Sarah laughs at the newborn manifestation of the promises of the Lord, then I will too. Grief is real. It is intense. But what is more real, what is more intense, what is eternal is the hope of Christ, the drying of tears, the new heaven

and new earth, the reuniting with Daisy, the final con-
quering of death. When I am pressed down, these truths
pull me back up. They are air to lungs submerged nearly
too long.

Don't miss out—don't trade inward thinking, skep-
ticism, lies, and emotion for truth and joy. We are so
prone to giving up the real for the perceived. One epic
way we miss out on life and focus on untruth is with
social media. Like many other things that can be good
if they're not exalted into an idol, social media is something that I don't partake of right now. Some have issues
with alcohol. Others have made their home a god, and
still others elevate entertainment or food or shopping or
beauty treatments or exercise. Any of these things can be
good if kept in check with wise boundaries, but they can
also quickly steal joy when they spin out of control. For
me, right now, it's social media.

I discovered this back in 2012, when we spent another
summer in hospitals seeking treatment for Daisy. She was
hurting and crippled from all the surgeries, treatments,
and chemo, and things were unsettled and frightening.
Plus, being in the hospital just stinks. Bad.

I'd never had a Facebook account but did have
Instagram at the time. If you have an account, you know
it's like crack in your veins. You scroll through people's
pictures, eyes rolling back in your head, numb at the
sight of so many people doing so many things. Things
you can't do. Things like going to the beach with friends.

Like barbecuing with family. Like not worrying about their kids dying from cancer.

And so the crack that entered my veins poisoned me. It drove my self-focus, it fed my self-pity, and it fueled my discontent. One day, out of sourness and resentment, I posted the view from Daisy's hospital room in LA, where we were waiting to harvest her stem cells. I was secretly wishing for the rest of the world to stop and notice our rotten lives, and hoping for some sympathy. It was then that I realized I was becoming jealous of other people's apparently easy lives. I wanted to be anywhere but where I was, to live anyone else's life but mine. And it was wrong. I was convicted. I felt God saying, "This is your life, the one I gave you. Be present, feel it, walk through it with me. Don't miss it."

Thank you, Jesus, for lifting my head, for showing me something that was taking from me, not giving. Thank you, Jesus, for exposing an unhealthy habit, for helping me cut it off, for replacing it with joy and the beauty of caring for another. I chucked Instagram that day and never looked back.

From now on, I only want to live my own life, not salivate after the lives of others. I want to relinquish what I wish my life looked like and relish what it is. I want to be all there; I want to be all-in. I want to be grateful and aware and responsible and respectful, and if I can't do that while scrolling past everyone else's posts, then peace out. Later. Don't let the door hit you on the way out.

God has so much for us when we are present. Lovely little gifts he gives us on a daily basis. What is hindering you from opening these gifts? From seeing them and snapping them up and trying them on right then and there? Whatever it is, get rid of it. Don't look back.

Because I ditched Instagram, I became aware of so much else. I saw things I never could before when I was so busy comparing my life to everyone else's. My heart was in such an open state, reaching out and grateful to God. We didn't know that the trip we were about to take to Israel would be the most soul-molding time of our lives. It was our last good time ever with Daisy. I was so grateful to have left Instagram behind beforehand, to have been able to enjoy each moment completely engaged. We made memories purely for ourselves. As gnarly and scary and uncomfortable as it was, the trip was a gift. A gift I took and opened and kept for myself without sharing with those to whom that gift was not given.

We, in our last few months with Daisy, were fully present. We were hurting and wrecked and questioning, of course, but we were all-in with both feet. We lived the life God had given us. We put on the running shoes because we didn't want to miss the race. Regardless of the sadness and stress, it was the most incredible time of our lives.

Last week I saw a woman wearing a shirt that said "Bloom Where You're Planted." I loved that. Sometimes I see a big flowering plant bursting out of a crack in the sidewalk and marvel. It appears that it is indeed possible to bloom wherever the Farmer has planted you. You might be planted in a sea of concrete, unexpectedly breaking through what was thought to be stronger than you. Or you might be planted on a windy hillside, roots exposed, growing lopsided from the struggle to survive. Some are planted in English gardens, amid beauty and abundance, drinking freely the water that gives generous life. Yet others fight for existence among a whole crowd of opposition, riddled with holes from the pests that are sucking their lifeblood.

I can't decide where I've been planted. Sometimes I think I'm in that lush English garden, water showering down on me in gentle abundance, surrounded by displays of beauty and life. Yet other days I feel I'm that anemic, cliff-dwelling tree, fighting every element against my ability to thrive, battling a constant barrage of hostility. Perhaps it's both. Both are a blessing to their environment. Both have purpose and beauty and are life-giving to their surroundings.

Just as I was all-in while we fought for Daisy's life, I have discovered how to be all-in when mourning her life. Shall I not laugh and play and nuzzle my daughter with the fawn curls and olive skin, because the one with the blond mermaid hair and sprinkling of freckles is gone? Shall I not honor God and enjoy all his gifts even if some are only given for a short while?

You can believe something is real, but unless you cross over it means nothing. Remember how my pastor said that what you do is what you believe? James said faith without works is dead. I'll show you my faith by my works— and sometimes that work is the simple act of choosing joy, choosing freedom, choosing to honor God through actions that spring from a sometimes harsh environment. I pray, Lord, show me the way of beauty.

When I am free to cross over and enjoy the goodness of family, of the earth, of friends and love and food and music and dancing, it glorifies God. It says, "I believe you. I agree with what you're doing." Crossing over draws out laughter, draws out worship, draws out trust, draws out love. Do you see it?

Twelve

UNTIL A WEDDING

Oh, she's adorable! Is she your first?" asked the friendly checker at Trader Joe's. The question snapped me to attention while Fifi squirmed and struggled in the grocery cart, determined not to leave a single chocolate bar on the display untouched.

As I attempted to be a gracious mother and speak sweetly to my little one while juggling yams and reusable bags and credit cards, I felt it. The lurch. The deer-in-headlights moment, feeling suspended in time. I had to make a split-second decision. *Do I give an honest answer and say she's my third? Do I lie to save face and say she's my second?*

On the fly I calculated what the relationship with the person was: Would I see them again? Did they know who I was? Would they later find out Daisy was gone and conclude I was delusional for what I was about to say? Because the question that always follows is how old the others are. Would it get weird? Should I tell them my middle child's body lies cold in a grave? I'd done that before, and it was awkward. Incredibly awkward.

So I did what felt like lying but was, actually, the true truth.

"No, she's my third."

"Surely not! You're so young and fit and fabulous! [Okay, that part was my imagination.] How old are the others?"

Deep breath.

"They are eleven and fourteen," I said.

I did it. I said something that was truth, though it could be construed as a lie. And I did it to escape the potential look of horror on a stranger's face and the stuttering and the gauche stories of her cat's bout with cancer or her grandma's death. And I didn't regret it.

While the checker chattered on about how much my baby's siblings must love her and help out so much at home, I got lost in the daydream of what it would have been like if Daisy had stayed on earth with us. She would have been eleven. She should have been eleven. It was not a lie; she is alive. She just lives somewhere that I can't see. I know it with all my heart. I am assured of this ethereal fact, this gorgeous mystery, because of what I have read in the Word of God, because I am acquainted with the One who conquered death. I have faith she is alive, faith I will join her, faith my tears are being collected and treasured, eventually to be wiped away.

Faith is a peculiar thing. "Have faith," people say when they're hoping it rains. "Have faith," they say when you're up for a promotion. Or "Have faith," they say when your daughter is on her third cancer diagnosis, fighting for existence and at death's door. We throw the word around, featherlight, gaily at an afternoon tea. Or we grip hands covered in sweat and dust, looking deep into eyes whose light is waning. Sometimes *faith* makes me think of ruby slippers clicked together or fingers crossed. Or of scrunched-up eyes and the groaning sound you make when you're reaching for something that's just an inch too far away. That word holds the weight of hopes and dreams; it can be airy or religious, meaningless or deep. Faith and confusion seem to bleed together, running down until you aren't sure what it was supposed to look like in the first place.

Truth is, it's not all that confusing. Once we shed our American Christian culture, our personal experiences with erroneous faith healers, or any false ideologies we might have held or assimilated, faith is more clear, more lovely, more life-giving than we can imagine. The Bible defines *faith* as the "confidence that what we hope for will actually happen; it gives us assurance about things we cannot see" (Heb. 11:1). This, this simple definition, holds an entire world in the balance for me. I can close my eyes and feel Daisy's warm delicate hand in mine. I feel her velvety hair right underneath my chin, the way I held her on my lap thousands of times. I hold my breath expectantly, certain of her existence, of her aliveness in a place I cannot see. I have my foot lifted, arms out—my stance ready to enter into this wonderful place and catch her at any moment.

Mary, the brave lioness, the mother of Messiah, demonstrated so much of this faith during her pregnancy and birth, though her agreement to participate in the story surely brought bewilderment. It began with a bang: the heavenly messenger, the bright star, the choir of angels, the exotic royal gift bearers, all surrounding Mary like confetti shot high into the air, twinkling down all around her and casting a gilded glow.

But then . . . silence. Like a book slamming shut, perhaps a few dust motes lazily spiraling in no particular direction. Following this supernatural commencement came years of obscurity and quiet. After all the confetti had fallen and become dusty on the ground, wedged into cracks in the dirt road, Mary was doubtless wondering if she had heard correctly. Ahead were years of the mortal, years of the mundane, years of latent power mysteriously concealed in humanity.

Gone were the cosmic entourage, the perilous adventure soundtrack. All that was left was perhaps the methodical ringing of the hammer. The thighs-in-corduroy sound of the saw, the dusty carpenter clothing to wash, the low hum of a small town with its buying and selling and gossip and donkeys and rabbis. There probably wasn't even much bickering in the family with Messiah as the eldest keeping the others in line. Every day the sun rose, bread was made, hummus was mixed, oil was pressed, garments were mended, pigeons were sacrificed, the Torah was read, and the sun set. Mundane. Life.

Until a wedding. I have been thinking about the wedding at Cana lately. I imagine the place dotted with gorgeous stone-walled estates nestled among vineyards. Olive trees lined up in neat rows with silvery green leaves quivering in the breeze and small, uniform herds of plump, healthy animals grazing lush pastures. And the famous wedding.

I'm envisioning twinkling lights everywhere, torches and candles and hanging lanterns casting the soft, radiant light that causes guests to appear svelte, sultry, and better-looking than usual. Pillows spilling out invitingly around low tables for dipping dates in herbed goat cheese and honey languidly dripping from the comb, piles of earth-hued olives. Bronze chalices of wine next to steaming stacks of flatbreads and wide saucers of hummus, pooled in the center with olive oil, green and fresh.

And dancing. Lots of it. A completely raging party where there is nary a square inch of dance floor to spare, sweat flying, hair and skirts twirling and pulsing in time with the music. Elegantly embroidered fabrics draped luxuriously around the merrymaking, creating swooping ceilings and tents, fluid with the night air. Gorgeous. At least in my mind. I actually have no idea what it would have looked like! But what we do know is that there was wine. Jugs of it. And that at this particular wedding, it had run out (What a bunch of lushes!), causing a problem for the wedding host.

Now Mary, ever the proud mother, knew her Jesus could do something about this relatively unimportant yet public and present problem. I just love that. Mamas, don't we all feel like that about our sons? Especially firstborns.

We make them do their tricks, sing sweet songs, and play instruments for guests. We brag on their abilities; we showcase all their accomplishments. We are starry-eyed about them. And of course Jesus, being God and all, could fix anything!

What I find most interesting here is that this wedding took place before Jesus had started his public ministry. He had gathered his disciples and been baptized by his cousin John, but there were no miracles recorded yet. He appeared ordinary, as described in Isaiah 53:2: "There was nothing beautiful or majestic about his appearance, nothing to attract us to him." He didn't even have a wife. Average guy from an average family, from an average town.

So, after all this time, after such a mystifying and incomprehensible yet celebratory beginning, he lived an incredibly common life. Had Mary spent thirty years with Jesus just waiting? I'm sure he was a great kid and a hardworking tradesman, but a miracle maker? Considering the political climate and Jesus' lack of antagonism toward Roman rule, was she second-guessing his identity? Maybe she ate too much spicy lamb that night when Gabriel came, or maybe he was the product of a young imagination? I don't think so.

No, all those years she'd held on to the words of the Lord. She had pondered them. She had stored them up in her heart, and despite having never seen Jesus perform a miracle, that truth gave her the confidence to ask him to do something about the wine problem. The story is really so cute. She learned the wine supply ran dry, so she found him and said (in my imagination) in a womanly, read-my-mind sort of way, "They have no more wine."

Hint. Hint.

And he replied with, "Mom! Stop pressuring me!" Okay, no, that was my son. Her perfect son said, "Dear woman, that's not our problem. My time has not yet come." Jesus was telling her he was not super into it; the miracle show had not officially commenced.

Mary, ever human and a female human at that, ignored him and told the servants to do whatever he told them to do. Mary, you're too much! I'm secretly relieved at this. I mean, all that sacrificing and faith and suffering and blessed-among-women stuff. She was real, after all.

We know the rest of the story. Jesus had the servants fill six stone jars with water and then had them bring some to the master of ceremonies, who after sampling it for himself was astounded at the quality of what had been turned into wine. Kind of a puzzling miracle, if you ask me, but Jesus was an efficient guy. The result of this party-saving sensation? His glory was revealed, and his disciples believed in him. Rad.

You know what my personal opinion of all this is? Two things:

1. Jesus loved his mom so much that he was willing to bless her by taking care of this issue that was important to her, and

2. Mary's faith was solid.

She had no doubts about who her son was, even after all that time. She believed he was who he said he was and that he would do what he said he would do. Thirty years of carpentry and Passover meals and Roman occupation couldn't change that. She had been meditating on the things that revealed God was keeping his word to her. She had been watching his movements, from the virgin birth to Jesus astounding the religious teachers and students at the temple in Jerusalem as a twelve-year-old to the beginning of his ministry. All along the way she acknowledged the hand of God.

Mary, you knocked it out of the park again with your disregard for circumstances, your trust in God's plan, knowing the one can't affect the other. Again, she partnered with God, stepping out into uncharted territory with confidence.

Britt and I learned to do this during the years we fought for Daisy's life, recognizing the ways we knew God was there all along. We had to if we wanted to survive. We kept a list—not a list that showed all the victories or prayers answered exactly how we ordered them, so we could make tally marks on the scoreboard for the home team—our list showed something even better. Because when the answer to the prayer was no, when the road was rocky, when suffering didn't let up but instead increased, we didn't count those things against God's record. That would have been missing out on what was good, true, and beautiful: that he saw the way we held her hands while she endured painful treatment. That he was with us, right there in the sterility of hospital rooms, in the cover of darkness as we clung to each other and convulsed with lamentation, in the endless loneliness that sickness brings. That he comforted us, from the ways he spoke to us through Scripture and friends to the small miracles that gave us peace. Had we not recognized those things we would have drowned in despair. What a humbling thing to be seen by the almighty God. What a gift to say that we have seen him. Just a teeny bit of faith can hold up even the weariest arms.

We continue on in the same way now that she is gone. We have learned to reflect on the goodness of our lives, on the loveliness that surrounds. We have learned to accept in faith both God's blessings and the hardships, openhandedly receiving from him what he chooses to allow. And we have learned to wait. We wait for Jesus when it appears his power is latent, wait with him while the waves of sadness wash past. We wait in faith, anticipating future splendor.

It was faith that God credited to Abraham as righteousness. It was faith that freed the slaves. It was faith that gave strength to the weak. It was faith that held up many historical heads to plow through mountains of formidable obstacles. Faith raises the dead; faith says yes to God when he says no to our requests. Faith is the love note we give to God. It's the act, or rather the choice, that pleases him.

Let's take another look at how our biblical friends' faith resolves, starting with Sarah. Go back to Genesis, this time to chapter 21. True to God's word, Sarah indeed had a baby boy, Isaac. Can you just see her in her traveling desert nursery? Layers of sheepskins overlapping, white and resplendent on a bed covered by a breezy gauze canopy. Sarah and Isaac lying together face-to-face, her aging lips kissing his plump ones, her sinewy fingers caressing his, fresh and stubby. Sarah looking up in wonder at her husband, sharing the deepest joy with this flawed yet faithful man. I can see her eyes crinkling at the sides, inviting Abraham to cuddle Isaac with her. Theirs was a world of quiet wonder, of warmth, of fascination at the spectacle of life—a newborn baby.

Sarah's worn-out body carried fat new life, and the delight of the whole marvelous affair caused an outburst—this time of felicity. She said so wonderfully in verses 6–7, "God has brought me laughter. All who hear about this will laugh with me. Who would have said to Abraham that Sarah would nurse a baby? Yet I have given Abraham a son in his old age!" Sarah's laughter as she held that baby inspires me to laugh in enchanted expectation. She traded secret mocking for the gorgeous tinkling of the laughter of a well-loved child, for surprise and delight and belief.

Regardless of what things appear to be or what our expectations demand of us, we are being invited to openly enjoy the anticipation of goodness. First Corinthians 13:12 tells us,

> Now we see things imperfectly, like puzzling reflections in a mirror, but then we will see everything with perfect clarity. All that I know now is partial and incomplete, but then I will know everything completely, just as God now knows me completely.

As he knew Sarah, God knows us, hears us, and says there is beauty to come. We may not see it now, but it will come, as sure as Sarah's vintage arms held fat new life, sweet breath promised and delivered.

Not only did God turn her bitter laughter joyful, but Sarah also made it into the coveted "Hall of Faith" of Hebrews 11:

> It was by faith that even Sarah was able to have a child, though she was barren and too old. She believed that God would keep his promise. And so a whole nation came from this one man who was as good as dead—a nation with so many people that, like the stars in the sky and the sand on the seashore, there is no way to count them.

All these people died still believing what God had promised them. They did not receive what was promised, but *they saw it all from a distance and welcomed it*. They agreed that they were foreigners and nomads here on earth. Obviously people who say such things are looking forward to a country they can call their own. If they had longed for the country they came from, they could have gone back. But they were looking for a better place, a heavenly homeland. That is why God is not ashamed to be called their God, for he has prepared a city for them. (vv. 11–16, emphasis mine)

Do you see the goodness of God in all this? His plans were good. Because of Sarah's and Abraham's belief, there came a whole nation of people who looked to God despite their circumstances. God's plans were to bless and rescue and love, in ways above what we expect or even know to ask for. And did you notice how these saints saw from a distance? They put on the lenses of Scripture, the sharp, clear, extremely good promises of God, to see further than they could see on their own.

What about Bathsheba? Bathsheba chose to honor God in the face of nasty circumstances, becoming a woman of dignity who raised her son to become a wise king. One who penned books of wisdom in the Old Testament. She unknowingly became a pivotal figure in the ancient movement lifting up a woman's place in society, a shining star who not only lived it herself, but guides women across the ages toward a life of valor and excellence. Bathsheba saw from a distance, through tears and shame, her future as an influential queen—no longer pinned to her adulterous identity.

And Mary. Mary honored God's will for her life, faithfully raising Jesus up from newborn to radical rabbi, all the while a faithful follower. She honored the Son of Man after his resurrection as part of the early church and carried out his request by caring for the apostle John like a son. Mary's faith made her a crucial part of the gospel going forth; she saw from a distance how worthwhile it was to pour her whole life out before the Lord, an offering fragrant and pure. I can just see her, surrounded by grand-babies and disciples and liberated women, laughing and remembering the days when the real, living Son of Man ate at her table, under her roof. Her faith was a driving force behind the joy with which she lived out her remaining days, anticipating reunion with her beloved firstborn.

All three women trusted God with impossible lives, unable to see how it would turn out in the end but giving their everything with open arms.

The beautiful thing about every one of these stories is that it was all Jesus! The promises, the pulling through, the blessing, the miraculous. All him. And it's still all him today. He is the one doing amazing things, giving without limit, yet we are the ones who receive, who benefit.

I have every reason to laugh without fear of the future; I have every reason to enjoy beauty, to dance and sing and surf and ride horses and eat delicious food. Like my biblical sisterhood, I can choose not to stay in the place of idle sadness. I can choose to lift my head, receive the gift of God's renewing love, and move forward, pressing into his generosity. Because the grace of God is without limit, shall I not reach for all I can get of it, even when it's difficult to see?

Even though things in my life are far from perfect, and they never will be, I have learned to lean into the goodness of God as I wait in faith for his ultimate redemption. I have come to the conclusion that it does not glorify God to wallow in despondency like a pig in mud. If I actually, really believe that this life is not all there is, if I truly believe the Word of God, the laws and prophets and books of history, the love poetry, the letters from missionaries to the early church, if I truly believe the visions of future goings-on, the comforting healing words of love written in an extraordinary compilation of sixty-six books authored by the Holy Spirit through forty different writers over the course of fifteen hundred years, I have every reason to rejoice.

All these yeses, all this hope, all this fixing of our eyes on the Beautiful One has proven to be worth it. That is the simplicity and loveliness of faith. Sarah and Bathsheba and Mary were merely foreigners here on earth, and so am I, and so are you. We are just passing through, not planning on settling in, not planning on staying forever. Why would we? This is not our country! Like the heroes of the faith, we choose. We get to decide where we want to "live" and then live accordingly. In the passage above from Hebrews, it says the faithful could have chosen to go back to where they came from, but they didn't. And neither will I.

My country is heaven. My country is where my Redeemer has prepared an imperishable and marvelous place for me. My country is where I will be welcomed by loved ones with doors flung wide, hands in the air, and big kisses right on the lips. It's where I will confidently climb into Jesus' lap and lift my face to feel his soft beard that had once been plucked out for me. It's where I will put my fingers in his nail-scarred hands and marvel at being so treasured, so heroically rescued. It's where he will look me fiercely in the eyes and say, "It's okay now. You're safe here." It's where he will gently dry the tears. Pain and dying will be done away with, and my best little girlfriend, whom I have missed all these years, will run into my arms and I will kiss her freckles once again. It's where I will brush her hair and hold her tight and swim and play and fly with her.

It's where I will be full-hearted, mended completely. It's where love will be consummated in the most real way we will ever know, and we will be swallowed up by life. It's where I will tip my brand-new, splendid, heavenly head back and, while showing every tooth, laugh my loudest, my freest. The laughter won't end, the light won't be vanquished. In God's mercy I will receive imperishable crowns of life and rejoicing and glory and righteousness.

My country is a place where a river flows, clear as crystal, watering twelve trees that give fruit every month. It's where there are gates of pearl and streets of gold. My country is lit up by the light of Jesus, free from all evil, a strong fortress of grandeur held together by the Author of Life, the Originator of Beauty. And it's a place where I will belong. I will gloriously, fully, shamelessly, and completely belong.

This, dear ones, is something to laugh about in anticipation! There is one gorgeous wedding feast of the Lamb to come, and we will dance.

This is the stuff of life: Mountains and valleys. Births and deaths. Laughter and weeping. And in my life, because I was an enemy of God and he showed me mercy while I was yet a sinner, I want to do right by him. Paul told us in 1 Corinthians 7:

> Let me say this, dear brothers and sisters: The time that remains is very short. . . . Those who weep or who rejoice or who buy things should not be absorbed by their weeping or their joy or their possessions. . . . For this world as we know it will soon pass away. (vv. 29–31)

P31 girl was known for laughing without fear of the future, not sitting around crying about the past. She found a depth in suffering that made steady her confident steps heavenward. She was given so many good things to look forward to, and she wisely chose joy. There's no time to waste.

Real life is full of real people, and real people are messy. Bathsheba was messy. Sarah was messy. Even Mary was messy. We are undeserving and selfish. We screw up, we drop the ball, we blow it time and again. But here's what's so amazing about looking heavenward and choosing Jesus: It doesn't matter if you haven't been the perfect woman. It doesn't matter if you've been eclipsed by bitterness or marked by sin. It's never too late to say yes, to accept the gifts. It wasn't too late for Sarah or Bathsheba or even for me. And it's not too late for you.

This glorious future is not only for the Proverbs 31 girl who makes the rest of us look bad. It's for the hurting. The lonely. The bereaved, the grieving. It's for the woman who's hiding an abortion. For the woman who is in need of forgiveness, to be washed clean. It's for the one who has suffered abuse, who is going through divorce. It's for the girl who has tried to take her own life, for the one who cuts herself to feel something, anything. And for the one who is tuned out, numb, dead to the world. Goodness awaits you! Goodness awaits me! Come with me, jump in, and feel the warmth of anticipation, even in the cold and dark night.

Can we please laugh together? Can we please honor God, the Giver? If he gives ice cream, lick up the last drop as it runs down the cone and onto your arm. If he has given a warm day, let your skin soak up the sun until your tan glows. When he gives sweet memories, camp out there a little while, sweeping your soul with goodness. Let the food you eat not only nourish your cells, but let it be beautiful and delicious and flavorful and plentiful. Walk in the rain, splash in puddles, catch snowflakes on your tongue. Watch a spider spin a web. Explore the world with your preschooler, his hand in yours, sticky with peanut butter and fat with love. Draw eyeliner kitty cat whiskers on your six-year-old, then drink milk out of a saucer on the floor of the kitchen with her.

If he has given you babies to love, pour it on thick. Rock and sing and kiss and bless, in the same way your Abba pours out to you. The home you have been given, have fun making it pretty. Pick your neighbor's flowers, put up drawings made by tiny, unsteady fingers, and paint the walls hot pink! Let music ring throughout; let singing and prayers abound, flowing freely from grateful lips. If he has given you a friend, a mentor, or a little sister, revel in the gift of human hearts knit together by truth. Use your gifts, use your talents, and point to the One who gave it all.

Sometimes the goodness is right in front of our faces, and sometimes it must be unearthed, but it's there. This is life. It's strange and wonderful and terrible all at the same time. Feel free to laugh, and feel free to cry. Feel free to create and love and take chances in scary areas of your life, for we have the brightest future to enter.

One day about halfway through Daisy's fight, I found her sitting on her bed listening to music. Her boom box was playing the song "Lead Me to the Cross."

She sat there so thoughtful and still. In that moment my heart broke yet again for the thousandth time. She was completely bald. She was bone thin. She was tired and sick and quarantined from friends. My girl had every reason in the world to dwell on her circumstances, for they were all around her—they could be seen in the mirror and felt with every frail breath and with every swallow through a mouth filled with sores.

She looked at me with her lashless hazel eyes, white duvet billowing all around her. And with a determined look on her face she asked me, "Mom, you know what I think this song means?"

When your seven-year-old is contemplating worship lyrics, you had better lean in close and listen.

"Tell me, honey."

"I think it means I'm going to live if Jesus wants me to live, and I'm going to die when he says it's time to die. But right now, until then, I'm going to live. I can feel it in my bones."

This came from a girl who had everything she knew as a child taken from her. Health, time with friends, comfort, security. She knew she could die from her disease. And still she was a girl who loved Jesus, who bloomed where she was planted.

My girl showed faith. She also showed tears and

fears and disappointment like a real human, but she saw beyond. She knew Jesus was better than anything here on earth. She could see the gifts all around her, and she savored each one. Such wisdom, such childlike faith. Her hand was held out to Jesus to walk her through the worst, the darkest. And her eyes were on the prize.

I want to leave you with this, written in a letter from dear old Peter:

Now we live with great expectation, and we have a priceless inheritance—an inheritance that is kept in heaven for you, pure and undefiled, beyond the reach of change and decay. And through your faith, God is protecting you by his power until you receive this salvation, which is ready to be revealed on the last day for all to see. So be truly glad. *There is wonderful joy ahead*, even though you must endure many trials for a little while. These trials will show that your faith is genuine. It is being tested as fire tests and purifies gold—though your faith is far more precious than mere gold. So when your faith remains strong through many trials, it will bring you much praise and glory and honor on the day when Jesus Christ is revealed to the whole world. You love him even though you have never seen him. Though you do not see him now, you trust him; *and you rejoice with a glorious, inexpressible joy.* (1 Peter 1:3–8, emphasis mine)

Glorious, inexpressible joy. Laughter that is free from circumstance. Laughter that sometimes makes no sense. Laughter that is one of the most healing and wonderful and mysterious earthly gifts.

And so, I'll say like Sarah, who held God's perfectly gentle and joyous laughing promise in her arms, with eyes squinting and shoulders shaking, who knew?

ACKNOWLEDGMENTS

I've always wanted to write children's books. I absolutely never thought I'd write a book for the taller sort, but this one just kind of flew out of me. I wrote it for myself as much as for anyone else, but I want to first thank my readers for giving me a reason to really own the truths in this book. Because of you I walk a bit stronger, remember a bit more clearly just how to grab on to healing hope.

To Britt, you have loved me since I was a teenager. You told me then to never sell myself short, and because of you I have been able to do scary and wonderful things I never thought possible. You are a man of integrity, generous with everything you've got, and you still look good. Thank you for listening to me spout a random paragraph here and there, just so I can see you look at me with approval. That must have been exhausting! And don't worry, by the way. I won't tell anyone you cry when you read my writing.

To Isaiah, Daisy, and Pheodora Sunshine, you three

are the absolute most fabulous kids on the planet. Well, two of you are on the planet, anyway. It's supereasy to love you. Isaiah, you are beyond. I admire the young man you are becoming: brave, generous, wise, kind, strong, and adventurous. Thanks for being so sweet when I make the same author jokes over and over. Daisy, your bravery on earth will always be astounding to me. You gave me eight of the loveliest years of my life. I can't wait to see you in heaven. Fifi, you're a crazy nut job and a total gift. You burst into our lives like a ray of sunshine, and you make us laugh even while the tears fall.

To my mom and dad, you have both let me be who I was made to be, never forcing anything and always loving me. Thank you for making me feel so accepted and encouraged, whether I am writing a book or finger painting with my babies. You're both pretty cool.

To Al and Terry, my other mom and dad. Thank you for welcoming me into your lives for the last twenty years and loving me like your own. From fly-fishing to flower arranging, you splashed beauty into my life. Thank you for the gift of your son and for the constant outpouring of love.

To all my friends, whether I've mentioned you in this book or not, you know who you are. Thank you for following hard after Jesus, for crying with me when it's time for mourning, and for cracking me up when it's time for laughter. I can't believe I get to live this crazy life with such solid women. You all make it that much more fun.

To Leigh Anne, true friend and tough coach. You pushed me to do better, to not give up, to go big or go back to bed. Thank you for your sweet friendship and the hours you spent encouraging me on the phone. Oh, and for all the best sayings ever. Shocking!

To Don, my friend first and agent second. You have shown me so much kindness for so many years now. Thank you for all the therapeutic phone calls, for loving my family, and for knowing I was a writer before I ever did. You and Brenda are truly wonderful. And shout out to Cammy too! Thank you all for loving Daisy.

To Jessica, my editor. You crawled inside my head for many months and helped me shape a bunch of thoughts into a real live book! You read my rough, therapeutic writing and helped me trim some fat (thanks for not judging!). You made this book so much better with your sharp eye. Thank you for seeing the potential, for picking me. I am lucky to work with you, and I value your friendship!

To the team at Thomas Nelson. Thank you for rooting for me. I know you see a lot of proposals and I consider it no small thing to work with you. It's so fun to have the little house on the spine of my book!

To all who read the *Pray for Daisy* blog and loved our family through Daisy's fight for life. I am so moved by your kindness, faithful prayers, generosity, and all-around encouragement. You have been the hands and feet of Jesus to a suffering family. Thank you for loving a little girl into heaven and loving her family through sorrow.

And to Jesus. Because of you I have life, courage, love, freedom, joy, and strength. You are a dream come true. Thank you for being my friend, even while I was your enemy.

ABOUT THE AUTHOR

Kate Merrick is all the things on the back cover of this book. But in real life, she is a crazy friend, an inappropriately loud laugher, and will eat anything if it includes bacon, chocolate, avocado, or cheese. She has a knack for (mostly) unwittingly breaking rules at conferences, camps, and her kids' school, and lets her teenager ride his skateboard through the church foyer sans shoes. She likes being under water better than being above it and usually refuses to wear sunscreen. A nouveau hippie at heart, Kate has a fondness for her mom's blouses from the seventies, loves to cook food she grew and meat she raised, and she is one of those people who uses coconut oil for everything—like Windex. She embarrasses her teenager when she wears bell-bottoms and willingly lends her chandelier earrings to her toddler. She dances hard at weddings, opens the sunroof when she's driving, and still checks to see if her dress twirls. But, most of all, Kate never gets over the feeling of being wholly loved by God, who has given her not only his friendship, but every sweet thing in life.

To find more of Daisy's story and watch her memorial, visit Kate's blog at kmerrick.com/daisy/.